CONTENTS

90 0375331 8

UNIVERSITY OF P

An Introduction to Curriculum
for 3 to 5 Year-Olds

Viv Moriarty and
Iram Siraj-Blatchford

Education Now Books

Published by Education Now Publishing Co-operative
113 Arundel Drive, Bramcote Hills, Nottingham NG9 3FQ

Copyright © 1998 Viv Moriarty & Iram Siraj-Blatchford

British Cataloguing in Publication Data

A catalogue record for this book is available from the British Library

Moriarty, Viv
Siraj-Blatchford,Iram

An Introduction to Curriculum for 3 to 5 Year-Olds

ISBN 1 871526 38 8

Design and production: JSB for Education Now Books

Printed by Mastaprint Ltd., Sandiacre, Nottingham

Acknowledgements

We are grateful to a number of people who have encouraged us in the process of writing this book. A special thanks goes to Dr. Priscilla Clarke for her contribution to Chapter 5. Part of this Chapter is based on a short paper Iram and Priscilla produced after conducting a joint workshop for the National Children's Bureau in 1993 on issues of culture and language for children under five and those who work with them. We also want to thank Janet and Roland Meighan for encouraging us to write the book and believing in us in the process of doing so. Our particular thanks go to our partners, Les and John, for their unstinting support and encouragement. We are also indebted to the many centres (especially in the category of combined provision) whose children and staff have inspired us to write the book and from whom we have learnt such a great deal. Finally, any shortcomings in the text are entirely the responsibility of the authors.

V.M. & I.S-B.

Chapter 1

Background to the *Desirable Outcomes*

Rationale for a curriculum for under fives

The concern of this book is to reach those practitioners who are instrumental in implementing the *Desirable Outcomes*. The *Desirable Outcomes* are not a curriculum, but they are instrumental in defining some of the content of the curriculum for under fives. At the time of writing these are the early years educators in the full range of provision currently on offer for children who are under five in England and Wales. Scotland and Northern Ireland also have similar documents. Traditionally, it is women who have mainly staffed this sector; they are relatively low-paid and tend to have low status in society. Few are trained as teachers, many have vocational qualifications and others still are unqualified.

The book intends to address concerns raised in a recent study conducted by the authors. This study found some significant variance in attitudes towards the *Desirable Outcomes* in different nursery provision and the results suggested that the policies embodied in *The Next Steps* might be interpreted in different ways within the diverse sectors. More specifically, those in the private sector believed that the *Desirable Outcomes* were creating a greater consistency across settings, whereas those in education were less inclined to believe this. Similarly, those with different training and professional backgrounds expressed different concerns with, and interpretations of the *Desirable Outcomes,* that may effect how these are being put into practice (see Moriarty and Siraj-Blatchford, 1998).

It is the aim of this volume is to illustrate possible ways of planning and implementing a curriculum for children who are under five. Currently there exists the policy document entitled

Nursery Education Scheme: The Next Steps (SCAA, 1996), which outlines *Desirable Outcomes for Children's Learning*. This document formed part of the previous Conservative Government's reform of education across all sectors which admitted 4-year-olds. These reforms have been radical and have aimed to establish a free-market ideology in education. The 1992 the White Paper *Choice and Diversity: A New Framework for Schools* framed it thus:

> "More diversity allows schools to respond more effectively to the need of the local and national community. The greater their autonomy, the greater the responsiveness of schools" (DfE 1992, para 1.2).

Paradoxically, this has been coupled with a centralisation of control over educational institutions to Central Government through the Secretary of State for Education. The introduction of the National Curriculum in 1988 has been the means of regulating the education sector. The National Curriculum was revised following a report by Sir Ron Dearing and further revision is expected in the year 2000. The *Desirable Outcomes* will also be revised over the coming years with consultation beginning in Summer 1998.

Having concentrated for some time on the years of compulsory schooling, the previous Government turned to provision for children who are under five. In 1996 the Audit Commission was asked to investigate and report on provision for under fives in England and Wales. The results of this extensive investigation were published in the document *Counting to Five: Education of Children Under Five*. This document reported some of the research into the value of early years education and concluded that "Children's early educational experience is crucial for developing the socialisation and learning skills that they will need throughout their lives" (The Audit Commission, 1996, p.4). The report also outlined the different services available for children who are under five.   These services include:

- maintained nursery education (within the school system)
- reception classes in maintained primary schools
- private schools
- private day nurseries
- playgroups (often part of the voluntary sector)
- local authority day nurseries (regulated by the Department of Social Services)
- family centres (Department of Social Services)
- childminders

The Audit Commission, however, stated that these services had been "characterised by unevenness in access, effectiveness, quality and costs" (1996, p.30). The Commission recommended that the diversity of provision should be retained, as it allows parents of children under five to choose the most appropriate provision for their children. However, it also recommended that there be regulation of the "market of public, private and voluntary providers" (p.32). On 1 April 1997 the Government introduced a national voucher scheme for nursery provision, that had previously been piloted in three local authorities. Under this scheme, parents of children aged four years were given a voucher worth £1,100, which could be redeemed at registered provision. In order to register, a setting "would have to show that it is working towards a set of specified learning goals" (p.32).   These learning goals (or *Desirable Outcomes for Children's Learning*) were published in the document entitled *Nursery Education Scheme: The Next Steps* (SCAA, 1996) which has outlined Government "plans to provide, over time, a nursery education place of good quality for all four year olds whose parents wish to take it up" (p.3).   Participating institutions have had to provide information "about the extent to which the quality of provision is appropriate to the desirable outcomes in each area of learning" (p.3). Provision has also been inspected by the Office for Standards in Education (OfSTED) and the inspection reports outline how far a setting meets these *Desirable Outcomes*. This current government announced soon after its election that it would abolish the voucher scheme, although the *Desirable Outcomes* remain as part of legislation and there has been a stated commitment to the *Desirable Outcomes* and the inspection of provision by OfSTED Registered Nursery Inspectors to raise standards in a very diverse sector.

The *Desirable Outcomes* themselves describe areas of learning, which would enable children to move onto the National Curriculum requirements at five. The *Desirable Outcomes* are divided into six areas of learning: Personal and Social Development; Language and Literacy; Mathematics; Knowledge and Understanding of the World; Physical Development and Creative Development. These areas of learning were also identified in the Rumbold Report, *Starting with Quality* (1990) as appropriate for early years children, although some aspects identified in the Rumbold Report were left out of the *Desirable Outcomes* (see Siraj-Blatchford, 1998). The Rumbold Report itself followed the 1985 HMI Report which identified the role of the early years as being to provide "the first steps on the path into a relevant, coherent and integrated curriculum" (HMI, 1985, para 2.5). The document *Nursery Education: The Next Steps* (DfEE, 1996) has clearly demonstrated the relationship between the *Desirable Outcomes* and the National Curriculum via a set of tables, which show how the areas of learning link to Key Stage One of the National Curriculum. The *Desirable Outcomes*, then, echo the subjects of the National Curriculum and the requirements of the curriculum at Key Stage One and the document is clearly set within an educational context.

There is also another strand present in the framing of the *Desirable Outcomes*, based on the theories of developmental psychology. The text of the *Desirable Outcomes* makes reference to the developing abilities of children and the importance of practical activity and the physical environment to stimulate learning in children. These learning theories have had legitimacy in the educational field and have developed from the work of such theorists as Piaget, Vygotsky and Bruner. Whilst in recent years there has been less emphasis placed on these theories in initial teacher education courses, some research suggests that primary and nursery teachers continue to refer to them. The work of these theorists has remained important in other child care and education courses, such as the Diploma in Nursery Nursing, the Certificate in Nursery Nursing and the National Vocational Qualification in Child Care and Education. These issues are significant because they further frame experience for the under-fives within an educational framework and thus, seek to unify an apparently disparate sector and place early years provision within a learning and education framework. There is some evidence to suggest that other settings may maintain different frameworks based on other ideologies. The *Desirable Outcomes* are therefore interpreted as a means for setting a minimum standard of education as a basic entitlement for every child. Siraj-Blatchford (1998) has shown how this can be built on to offer a fuller and more flexible curriculum based on the Rumbold Report's nine areas of educational experience and framed within an early childhood philosophy which values individual children and their interests as an important element of curriculum construction.

This book does not aim to propose a rigid curriculum based on the *Desirable Outcomes*, but rather to consider a number of curriculum models in conjunction with the *Desirable Outcomes* and to offer ways of framing a curriculum whilst taking into account the differences in locality and contexts in which early years settings and practitioners operate. Cross-curricular themes are also considered as part of a curriculum framework, using such themes as Citizenship and there is exploration of the fostering of social skills and emotional development in young children. There will also be presented ways of planning an early years curriculum, to benefit all children in a setting, including those who may have Special Educational Needs. This book includes practical models for assessing early years children's abilities and valuing their achievements. There will also be consideration of continuity and progression to Key Stage One of the National Curriculum and links with the children's parents and carers.

The final sections of the book consider research concerning the implementation of educational policy and investigations into the assessment of quality of early years settings. This material is included to enable early years practitioners to have a clearer insight into their own practice and consider ways forward for their own setting. In conclusion, it is hoped that this book will provide early years practitioners with a guide to planning the curriculum in their early years setting, whilst also offering a theoretical perspective on that curriculum. A tailor-made curriculum within the framework of good early years care and education is vital if we are to avoid a 'top-down' pressure of the National Curriculum as was suggested by Sylva, Siraj-Blatchford and Johnson (1992) in their study of curriculum in Social Services and Education nurseries. The *Desirable Outcomes* framework does not impose *how* early years practitioners educate young children nor do they restrict *what* can be taught beyond *outcomes*.

Chapter 2

Integrating Care and Education

Research evidence supporting integration

The commitment of central government to the principle of nursery education dates back beyond the Plowden Report. However in 1972 the White Paper *A Framework for Expansion* recommended that nursery education should be extended and available for 50% of three-year-olds and 90% of four-year-olds. This document clearly positioned nursery provision within an education ideology, but failed to provide legislation to expand provision.   At this time, research into nursery provision concentrated on the compensatory nature of nursery education. Since the 1970s there has been a shift in research focus to concentrate on whether nursery education makes a difference to long-term educational achievement.   The most prominent of these has been by Schweinhart, Barnes and Weikart (1993) into the High/Scope programme, which has found long term benefits to children who underwent this nursery programme.   Further consideration of this model is made later in this chapter. The first study to look at pre-school effectiveness in England is currently underway and will report initial findings in 2001. The Effective Provision for Early years Education (EPPE) Project is based at the University of London Institute of Education and funded by the DfEE.

Despite evidence that high quality nursery education affects long term achievement positively and a multitude of Education Acts since 1988, nursery education has not been high on government agendas for funding.   In 1992 Department of Education statistics reported that 38% of three-year-olds and 56% of four-year-old in England were in publicly funded nursery classes or Reception classes.   Whilst the Department for

Education and Employment has responsibility for nurseries in the education sector, the Department of Social Services had responsibility for monitoring day care and other provision, and for granting registration under the Children Act. These departments have different structures and priorities and differing ideologies. Penn (1994) and Sylva, Siraj-Blatchford, Johnson, (1992), have researched these aspects.

These studies have indicated that staff in different sectors of early years provision have different values and priorities for the curriculum which they offer. They found that staff in local authority day nurseries and in the social services sectors made little reference to educational or pedagogical concepts and that activities for the children were poorly planned, limited and dominated by adults. Generally, these nurseries were framed in a welfare ideology, where caring for the children was a priority for the staff. Penn states that the current policy for nursery education "implies that there is little difference in practice between the education practices of state provided nursery education and privately provided day-care and that those distinctions in quality which may exist can be addressed by a tightening of inspection standards" (p.36). In Moss and Penn (1996) day nursery staff and teachers working in nursery schools and classes were asked "to sum up the principle which informed their work" (p.38). For the teachers the main aim was to promote children's learning, with the curriculum as "central to this purpose" (p.38). The day nursery staff, however had a "more diffuse view of their purpose - caring for children, promoting children's development, supporting parents, providing information - and they see themselves as having many tasks...the curriculum is peripheral" (p.39).

Between 1980 and 1991, there was an expansion of provision in some sectors. Sylva and Moss (1992) reported that playgroup provision had expanded by 16%, private provision by 259% and childminding by 137%. During the 1980s the Government also made attempts to shift responsibility for early years provision to employers, and gave incentives for employers to establish work place crèches for their employees. However, provision in different sectors continues to vary and staff training varies also. Teachers in nursery settings within the Education Departments of Local Authorities must have a teaching qualification (equivalent to four years higher education study post 18). All nurseries in this sector must be staffed by at least one qualified teacher. Nursery nurses (have two years post-16 further education training) account for a large number of educators in nurseries in the education sector and in the social services sector (approximately 14,000 in the UK in these sectors, source, Moss and Penn, 1996, p.100). Nurseries in the other sectors have no such requirements. In the private and voluntary sectors there are no legal requirements for the training of educators and local authorities are free to impose their own regulations. These vary throughout the United Kingdom and reliable information on qualifications held by staff in these sectors has been difficult to obtain. Training of staff and their status within the sector may make a difference to their beliefs and values and perceptions of the *Desirable Outcomes*, and effect the implementation of the policy. Just recently, services for under-fives have been brought into the Department for Education and Employment. The aim is to unify much of what comes under Health and Social Services into one umbrella department and therefore aid coherence in service provision.

Working conditions within the sectors also vary enormously. Although teachers may work extended hours, their contact time with the children will be limited by the length of the school day and the length of school terms. The average length of time that teachers and nursery nurses in the education sector have contact with the children is between 25 and 30 hours per week, with twelve weeks holiday. For teachers in the education sector there is a national pay scale and the opportunity for career advancement through promotion. Nursery nurses in the education sector do not have the same career opportunities. In private day nurseries, contact hours for staff may be between 37-40 hours per week, and staff generally works within shift systems. They receive, on average, 3-4 weeks annual leave a year and there are few promoted posts within the sector. Rates of pay are generally less than their higher qualified teaching counterparts within education, although they may exceed the pay of nursery nurses within education, depending on levels of responsibility. Educators in the voluntary sector work an average of 5-15 hours per week and annual leave is unpaid. Rates of pay are very low (£2/£3 per hour) and similar to the rates of pay for a Childminder. Childminders work an average of 50 hours a week and may be working continuously, without breaks, throughout the day. (Moss and Penn, 1996, p.100). This information demonstrates the differences there are between the different sectors in terms of staffing, conditions and training requirements. There are also considerable differences between settings within each of the sectors, depending on local conditions and social factors.

The recent legislation effecting nursery education assumes that one universal policy can be adequately implemented across this diversity and the policy itself can be viewed as an extension of educational reform, which began in the mid-1980s. The Education Reform Act (1988) represented both a move towards the concept of the free market in education and, paradoxically, a centralisation of power to the Secretary of State for Education. As Ball (1994) has expressed it, the Education Reform Act brought a new economy of power, invested in curriculum, assessment, pedagogy and organisation. The concept of the free market has been a "major aspect of national politics ... for about the past 10 years" (Bash in Bash and Coulby, 1989 p.19). This ideology assumes that educational resources are distributed evenly throughout the market and potential customers are able to choose which service they purchase. "As a result, there is what is called a perfectly competitive market operating to the benefit of all without any need for state intervention" (1989, p.19). The concept of a voucher for education was part of the ideology of the market. The voucher, enabled consumers (parents in this context) to make a choice of nursery provision for their children. The ideology dictates that those services which offer the "most value for money are those which provide a given quantity and quality of service for the lowest possible cost" (Bartlett and Le Grand, 1993, p.14). Poor providers would, then, be driven out of business. The difficulties of applying the ideology of the market to education have been well documented (for example, Bash and Coulby 1989). One of the chief anomalies regarding the school sector is that parents have a legal responsibility to send their children to school and cannot therefore choose not to have their children educated. In turn, the school has a legal responsibility to deliver the National Curriculum, so that choice is limited and parents are not free to enter or leave the market as they wish. The term *quasi market* has been applied to education because no money changes hands during the consumer/provider transaction (Halpin and Troyna, 1994). This may not, however, apply to nursery education, which is not compulsory and which, theoretically, could offer choices between a number of providers.

Ideology and policy development
Bartlett and Le Grand (1993) have written that the "monitoring of quality also has to be an essential part of any quasi-market system" (p.25). Part of the monitoring of quality in the nursery education sector will be through inspections, the criteria being how far the setting is working towards the *Desirable Outcomes*. These, then, become an important vehicle for the nursery

education policy and implementation of the *Desirable Outcomes* will be important for the implementation of the policy itself. As part of the overall nursery education policy, the *Desirable Outcomes* represent an "authoritative allocation of values" (Ball, 1990, p.1). By this, Ball means that policy itself embodies the ideology and principles of the powerful groups in society. Ball continues "policies cannot be divorced from interests, from conflict, from domination or from justice" (p.1). In his analysis of policy in education, Ball has considered three issues. The first of these are the struggles between interest groups. In the nursery education context, these interest groups include the policy makers themselves, the staff working in the nurseries and parents. The second issue is the notion of correspondence between education and the economy. This is embodied in the funding for nursery education, latterly through vouchers. The third issue is the role of discourses. In this context, discourse may be defined as the narrative of the dominant group, embodying knowledge and power. The *Desirable Outcomes* are themselves a discourse, and a questionnaire survey carried out during the Spring of 1997 (Moriarty, 1997) seemed to suggest that meanings may not be shared and understood by those who will be charged with implementing the policy.

The nursery education policy, like the policies embodied in the Education Reform Act, represent structural changes. The educators in the settings, rather like teachers in schools, will have to implement the changes. Kosunen (in Carlgren, I. Handal, G and Vaage, S, 1994) has researched the effects of curriculum changes in Finland. In this study there was concern to discover teachers' interpretations of the curriculum and the method by which change and reform in education was being brought about. Kosunen has written "the idea that an education innovation can be put into practice by presenting teachers with a new list of objectives has often been implicit in curriculum innovations. The curriculum has been seen as an instrument of school reform and teachers as mediators between the curriculum and the intended outcome" (p.249).

Research studies within the field of educational policy implementation have traditionally followed one of two models. The first of these is the *top down* model, where research has concentrated on the identification of the conditions which would enable the policy objectives to be translated into practice. This model has its limitations, as it considers policy formulation and policy implementation as two distinct phases, making the process a linear and hierarchical one. The second model is the *bottom up* model, which emphasises the importance of the organisations (schools) and actors (teachers) in their interaction with consumers (children and parents). In this model, it is argued that it is these actors "who determine the extent to that policies are rendered effective" (Fitz et al, 1994). This model also has its limitations as it can overlook larger factors which may influence the people who are acting upon the policy, such as the social issues involved in those actions as well as the values and perceptions of the implementers.

In contrast to both these models, Ball and Bowe have replaced them with the concept of policy generated and implemented "within and around the educational system" (Ball and Bowe, 1992, p.100). By this, Bowe and Ball mean that there is a balance between the policy makers' power to disseminate policy and the practitioners' capacities to interpret policies. Thus, practitioners "are conceptualised as meaningfully interpreting, rather than simply executing, policy which has been 'handed down'" (Fitz et al, 1994 p.60). The key to this process for Bowe and Ball is the relationship between the practitioner and the policy text, which in the current context is *The Next Steps*. As Bowe and Ball write: "'Making sense' of new texts leads people into a process of trying to 'translate' and make familiar the language and the attendant embedded logics" (Bowe and Ball, 1992, p.11).

Further, these texts "carry with them both possibilities and constraints, contradictions and spaces", (Bowe and Ball, 1992, p.15). All this implies that there is an interactive relationship between the practitioner and the policy, via the policy documentation. The generation and implementation of policy are no longer viewed as separate moments, but part of a continuum. Bowe and Ball assert that teachers are, in fact, effectively rewriting policy as they engage and respond to the text itself. Engagements and responses will depend on practitioners' understanding of the changes that are taking place and on the teachers personal histories and the local conditions in which they work. Bowe and Ball have assumed that teachers are not a homogeneous group to whom policy is "done", but who themselves act upon policy. With the wide variety of early years practitioners working in the early years sector, this aspect may be even more pronounced. Moreover, the introduction of the National Curriculum had seemed to weaken the teachers' professional confidence and lowered morale. This has also been documented in relation to early years teachers. Where the National Curriculum, associated reforms and research studies undermined their practice (Siraj-Blatchford, 1993)

In the United States of America, Spodek (1987) has conducted research into the thought processes of early years teachers' decisions. Spodek stated: "Teachers' actions and classroom decisions are driven by their perceptions and beliefs. They create conceptions of their professional world based upon their perceptions of reality and their beliefs of what is true" (p.197). Spodek used observational and interview material to ascertain, amongst other things, whether there was a system of constructs and beliefs common to classroom teachers in early years environments. Whilst Spodek discovered "significant patterns of thought that distinguished each teacher" (p.203), most of the findings indicated that teachers were "more thoughtful about management concerns than about learning and development" (p.205). These early years teachers also expressed a "concern for helping children adapt to the group and becoming involved in classroom activities" (p.206). Beyond these, Spodek found a large diversity of thought and few commonalties. There were "few thoughts about common goals, about common values, about common theories, and about common procedures" (p.207). In a later study, Spodek (1988) researched kindergarten teachers' beliefs and found that they, too, emphasised classroom management but placed less emphasis on play and more on work in order to socialise the children into school. These teachers tended to base their theories on personal values and experiences. Where a common core of thought may be found and the principles of early years education are agreed upon, practice may still be different. Buchanan (1995) compared Montessori nurseries, traditional nurseries and pre-school playgroup provision. Educators in all these settings believed that children were active in their own learning. A common aim of all staff was to develop the child as a whole person, but practice itself was at variance in these different settings despite agreement of aims.

Empirical studies have been conducted with teachers who have philosophies that are contrary to policy, mostly in the United States of America. Research conducted by Hatch and Freeman (1988) in Ohio concerned the implementation of a curriculum programme for early years children. There was some concern by the authorities in Ohio that this programme was not being followed in the early years settings. Hatch and Freeman (1988) interviewed staff in the early years settings and found that their beliefs were in conflict with the programme, which they perceived as too academic and based on principles of behaviourism. The findings of Hatch and Freeman's study were that "individuals who work in kindergartens and are responsible for them may be implementing programmes that they do not believe best serve the needs of young children" (p.158). The Kindergarten programmes were "skill based, highly structured, academically focused, and based on a direct instruction model" (p.158), which were defined by the researchers as having a "behaviourist orientation to learning and development" (p.158). The researchers further found that nearly 67% of the individuals interviewed expressed different principles on which they based their teaching methods. 50% expressed maturationist principles (defined as emphasising the role of biological change in development and learning) and 50% expressed interactionist principles (defined as emphasising the importance of the interaction of the individual with his or her environment). Hatch and Freeman have called this dilemma a "philosophy-reality conflict" (p.151) that has "implications for educational policy" (p.163).

Other studies conducted both in Britain and in the United States of America have attempted to highlight the beliefs and values of early years practitioners. Whilst there has been a general agreement that these are important, there is little consensus over how they might be important and what these beliefs and values might be. Charlesworth et al (1991) investigated "the relationship between the beliefs and practices of teachers of young children" (p.18) using a questionnaire and observational data in order to "gain some insight into the congruence between the teachers' perceived practices and those actually used in the classroom" (p.23). Charlesworth et al discovered that most of the teachers researched thought that appropriate beliefs were important and "included some appropriate activities fairly frequently" (p.32), but also found that developmentally appropriate beliefs were not always acted upon in practice. Whilst the notion of "child-centredness" as a principle for action was found to be a common theme, evidence has suggested that interpretations of what this means in practice differ widely. Whilst researchers such as Hurst (1991) have called for a defence of the child-centred curriculum, other studies have found a wide variance in interpretations of a "child-centred developmental approach".

This aspect may have implications for the introduction of a curriculum in those settings. Pound (1989) has attempted to research curriculum priorities with twenty four nursery teachers in England, using a schedule introduced by Bussis et al (1976) for identifying the priorities teachers operate under when constructing the curriculum for children. The most obvious and perceptible forms of curriculum Bussis referred to as "surface content" (p.50). There is also a deeper level, referred to as "organising content" which consists of the learning priorities and concerns that the teacher has. These learning priorities then divide into cognitive and personal/social priorities and numbered seventeen in total. The priorities the teachers had were inferred from interview data. Pound used these curriculum priorities and assigned teachers' beliefs to these via interview data. Overall, both in Pound's and Bussis' studies, teachers claimed more cognitive priorities than social priorities for the curriculum. However, as Pound has written in the discussion to her paper, there is an "absence of agreed, articulated views of what curriculum actually means within nursery education" (Pound, 1989 p.88).

Despite these findings from research, there has been no explicit reference made to differences in ideology between settings and practitioners in any Government documents. On 4 July 1997 a consultation paper was launched for local authorities on the formation of early years development partnerships and early years development plans. Local Authorities had to produce Plans for developing Early Years Partnerships in their services by February 1998. These plans must "demonstrate how co-operation, collaboration and partnerships between local authorities and the private and voluntary sectors can be used to secure provision and to match the nature of those places to the needs of children and their parents" (DfEE, 1997, para 1). Moreover, the sectors are to be brought together "in a spirit of co-operation and partnership, building on existing good practice" (para 4). In addition, the first 'centres of excellence' settings were announced at the end of 1997 (Government press release, 21 October 1997). The document *Progress with Partnerships* (DfEE, 1997) concentrates on the practical measures to be organised when setting up an early years partnership and says little about curriculum or children's learning. There is a small paragraph in this document about the importance of *shared* values, however there is no explicit mention of what these values might be.

Integrated Nursery Centres
Moss and Penn state that early childhood services need to be placed "within a wider context" to encourage "widespread participation and increased awareness and understanding...[and] increase societal legitimacy for early childhood services" (Moss and Penn, 1996, p.148). The DfEE have given responsibility for the forming of partnerships to the Local Authorities, who must oversee and co-ordinate services for children in the early years. Guidance from the DfEE gives examples of partnerships between:
- early years settings and schools
- community nurseries and Local Authorities
- integration of early years services
- primary schools and private nursery schools
- special educational needs provision and mainstream provision

An example of a combined early years centre is Pen Green in Corby. Pen Green combines four main strands in its provision.

These are: community education; health resources; a family centre and adult education (Whalley, 1994). The nursery is for children under and over three, with extended day care and extended year provision. Additionally, the centre has a positive policy of integrating children with disabilities and runs an after-school club. The family centre offers support for parents in the community, whilst the health centre gives practical help by providing services such as family planning and vaccination clinics. Centres such as Pen Green aim to provide a more flexible and integrated service to the community and combine care and education.

Hillfield Nursery Centre in Coventry and the Dorothy Gardner Centre in London are some of the earliest combined centres, having been open since the early 1970s. Like Pen Green, both Hillfields and Dorothy Gardner Centre have been recognised as a Centres of Excellence by the Department for Education and Employment. At these Centres as well as nursery places, there is a drop-in facility for up to 25 children at each session. The rooms are laid out for children to engage in imaginative, manipulative and aesthetic experiences. Additionally there is an area for babies, based on heuristic play (Goldschmeid and Jackson, 1994). A staff member at the centre also arranges a weekly discussion group for parents. There is provision for children all year round and the nurseries have an extended day.

The benefits of this integrated and extended provision have been outlined by Siraj-Blatchford (1995). These advantages include the support and education they provide for parents within the community and the responsive nature of these centres to "the need for continuity of care and learning" (p.9). Whilst the above centres are an example of excellence as 'combined' services, generally, "services for children under five in the UK are...characterised by a serious lack of co-ordination, too much diversity and paucity of provision" (p.3). These issues must be addressed at local authority level and the forming of early years forum in authorities may be the beginning of the process of combining centres.

Curriculum principles

When heads and managers of early years settings were questioned by researchers, knowledge of child development was considered to be "the single most influential factor in the professional development of practitioners who work with the under-8s" (Blenkin, Hurst, Whitehead, Yue, 1995, p.3). Also, when asked to describe a quality curriculum for this age group there was "a remarkable consensus among practitioners" (p.4), in which there was described a broad curriculum, with an emphasis on "the social curriculum and the personal ethos of early education" (p.4). While this consensus may have been discovered in this study, other studies have found that the articulation of these aims into practice has been less than satisfactory.   Examples   include   Spodek's   study   (1987) conducted in North America, in which he found "few thoughts about common goals, about common values, about common theories and about common procedures" (p.207). Similarly, in the United Kingdom, Buchanan's study (1995) of Montessori nurseries, traditional nurseries and early years playgroups found that although staff had a common aim to develop the child has a whole person, practice was at variance. Again in the United Kingdom, Pound's study (1989) discussed an "absence of agreed, articulated views of what curriculum actually means within nursery education" (p.88). It seems important, then, to establish these aims and articulate them fully.

Writers such has Blenkin and Kelly (1996) have also attempted to articulate a curriculum based on developmental principles. The stated aim in this case is the "widening of every person's horizons of appreciation and understanding, the maximisation of everyone's potential, the development of everyone's powers of self-direction, autonomy, understanding and critical awareness" (p.10). Furthermore, these principles imply an active involvement in learning by the participants, "so that the concept of active learning is a crucial element in this theory" (p.11). In a similar vein, Isenberg and Brown in Isenberg, Renck, and Jalengo (1997), define 'development' as "dynamic change over time" (p.31). Raines in the same book considers developmentally appropriate practice and an early years curriculum. Raines cites Piaget's theory of the construction of knowledge as the basis for such an approach, whilst taking into account the Vygotskian perspective of children learning in a social context and with adult mediation. The challenge for adults within this model is to "focus on what skills are learned as children construct knowledge" (Raines in Isenberg et al, 1997, p.86). This will mean that the developmental needs of the children are the most important part of the curriculum and that any decisions made about curriculum content must be made with reference to the individual children concerned. However, as Blenkin and Kelly (1996) express it "it is not necessary to lose sight of the fact that there are certain bodies of knowledge, certain kinds of understanding and certain cognitive skills which it would be irresponsible, and in fact impossible to ignore in the planning of educational provision" (p.13). These will be based in culture and have a social basis. Martin Woodhead (1996) argues that whilst early years practitioners should consider each child's individual needs, this must be realised in a social context. Thus practice should also be "contextually appropriate", and based on "local variations of children's experience, growth and change" (p.69). Moreover, early years programmes should be relevant and complimentary to the experiences of the community in which the setting is based.

The *Desirable Outcomes* may, then, be seen as these culturally and socially based understandings and skills which need to form part of the experiences of children in early years settings. The *Desirable Outcomes* can be viewed as a framework on which to construct a socially and individually meaningful curriculum for each early years setting. By considering other models of curriculum, it may be possible to construct an early years programme that takes into account local variations.

Some Models of the Curriculum
Te Whariki: The Woven Mat

In New Zealand there has been much work done on creating an appropriate curriculum for the early years of education. Here, the metaphor (taken from the Maori language) of Te Whariki (woven mat) has been used to describe the curriculum framework which is to be the guiding threads of the early years programme in each setting. Each early years centre will "weave its own curriculum mat, and create their own pattern from features and contexts unique to them, their children and their community" (Carr and May, 1993). The curriculum framework includes four principles, which are: empowerment; holistic development; family and community; relationships. In addition there are five strands, which are: well-being; belonging; contribution; communication; exploration. Goals give clear directions for learning programmes and outline learning outcomes which identify a set of knowledge, skills and attitudes children should have the opportunity to develop.

High/Scope

The High/Scope early years approach begins from the principle that "children learn actively and construct their own knowledge" (Macleod, 1989, p.33) and that this knowledge comes from their personal interaction with the world. This leads to a curriculum that emphasises children learning through direct experience with real objects and from applying logical thinking to this experience. The daily routines in a High/Scope curriculum will consist of the cycle of plan, do and review. During planning, children decide what activity they will engage in for the session. Once the 'do' part of the routine is complete, the children recall what they have done during review time. Children's progress is assessed around 58 key experiences in child development, which are grouped around eight categories (Hohmann, Barnet, Weikart, 1979, updated in 1995). These eight categories are: active learning; language; experiencing and representing; classification; seriation; number; spatial relations and time.

A setting organised to provide the High/Scope experience will be divided into interest areas to promote active learning and specific kinds of play. The materials must be accessible to the children to allow independence. The adult's role is to participate as a partner in the children's activities and there is an emphasis on positive interaction strategies, allowing children to share control and form authentic relationships with other children. In addition, the adult must support children's learning and extend it by helping problem solving.

The adults assess children using anecdotal notes of children's significant behaviours during activities. There is also a more formal observation record, which is used to help with forward planning. The High/Scope programme has been reviewed regularly through a cohort of 123 black Americans born in poverty and identified as being at high risk of failing in school. When these children were 3 and 4 they were randomly divided into an early years programme group who received a High/Scope approach and extensive parent outreach and those who had no such programme. At the age of 27, the participants were interviewed and other data were analysed. The High/Scope group was found to have had fewer arrests, had a higher economic status, had performed better academically and had more of a commitment to marriage (Schweinhart, Barnes, and Weikart, 1993). This evidence seems to suggest that a High/Scope programme can positively influence children's lives.

Reggio Emilia

Reggio Emilia is a district in Northern Italy where there are currently 22 early years settings for children aged 3 to 6 years, that offer full day care and social service support for families. The teacher Malaguzzi had been instrumental in developing the Reggio approach. He believed that learning happens in a social context and that collaboration between adults and children is crucial for the growth of the individual. This reflects the theoretical perspectives of Vygotsky and Bruner, with the emphasis on the child's construction of knowledge and understanding, with adult support. Each early years setting consists of three classrooms, one each for three-year-olds, four-year-olds and five-year-olds and an art studio. Each room has two co-teachers and a resident art specialist who all play an integral role in the children's learning. A Pedagogista, or child development specialist, co-ordinates the teachers from several schools. The principles of the Reggio approach are: parental involvement; an aesthetically pleasing environment; collaboration toward common goals.

The curriculum is not in linear form but is adapted to the interests of the children. Teachers transcribe tapes of children's conversations and discuss the content of them in order to plan the next step in the curriculum. 'Documentation' practices are considered important for the children's learning and this process is focused on children's experiences and thoughts that may arise in the course of their work. Display forms an important part of documentation. Children are encouraged to express their understanding through symbolic representation such as drawing, sculpture or writing, which are then discussed and displayed. These ways of representing experiences and understandings are termed "languages" (Edwards, Gandini and Forman, 1993), and the teacher must be prepared to provide a rich environment and a selection of materials for children to use.

These different models of curriculum all depend on theoretical perspectives which are overt and stated as part of the principles on which early years practice is to be undertaken in different settings.   Whilst these principles are to be common across different settings, locally these can be adapted to suit each early years setting or nursery and the children and families it serves. The next chapter considers how these theoretical perspectives may be developed in a curriculum based on the *Desirable Outcomes*.

Chapter 3

Planning the Curriculum

Long, medium and short-term plans

Planning must "involve clear perceptions about the various objectives of the curriculum and how different activities can contribute to their achievement" (Rumbold Report, p.10, para 76). Whilst the *Desirable Outcomes* express a set of skills and understandings which are now generally considered appropriate for early years children to acquire, it is important that these are given meaning in each setting, so that experiences for the children can be contextualised. Planning the curriculum needs to be at three levels: long term, medium term and short term.

Long term plans are the way any early years setting can express its ethos and values and give indications of how these might be implemented in practice. These long term plans will be agreed by all staff and discussed with parents and the management committee or governing body and should present a broad and balanced approach to the curriculum that will be on offer. At Pen Green Centre for under fives and their families in Corby there is a strong theoretical perspective based on the work of Chris Athey (1990). Working from the theories of Piaget, Athey considers that children have 'schemas' which determine the way they relate to the world. Some children may be 'transporting', others 'connecting' and others 'enveloping'. According to Whalley (1994), at Pen Green staff observe individual children's schemas and provide appropriate ideas and materials to extend the children's learning and thinking. The main aim of the curriculum plan at the Centre is to work with children's interests and self-chosen activities and to develop the children's own skills of negotiation and decision making. Another important aspect of the Centre's work has been helping children to cope with threatening behaviour from adults and other children and a programme has been devised to enable children to express their feelings.

Greengables Nursery in Edinburgh has a long term plan which concentrates on literacy skills and the management of children's behaviour based on valuing and praising children.   At the Patmore Centre in London, the curriculum is planned and monitored using five areas of development and in close consultation with the parents of the children who attend the nursery. Here, there is emphasis on the language used by adults to children and to each other and the developing of positive relationships within the nursery. The staff has written a set of guidelines for good practice, which begins with the statement: "Children are individuals and need respect. They have the right to hold their own views and should be encouraged to do so" (Makins, 1997, p.36).

It is the responsibility of each nursery setting to consult within the nursery and with the parents and the children themselves to decide what is important for that setting and how to devise long term plans around the important issues. These will then become a contextually appropriate framework for the nursery setting that will be based on local issues and will demonstrate how the universal elements of the *Desirable Outcomes* will be made relevant to the children and families in the nursery setting. This will go some way to fulfilling the criteria for 'contextually appropriate practice' outlined by Martin Woodhead (1996). Similarly, Spodek and Saracho's (1991) work on early childhood curriculum highlights that the curriculum should reflect the social values of the children and translate these into concrete experiences, so that the "structure, process and content" (p.x) will be unique to each early years setting. This principle is also the basis of the New Zealand early years *Te Whariki* curriculum. In *Te Whariki* goals to be realised by the children are defined, but the outlining of learning programmes is left to the individual setting. However long term planning is to be achieved, there should be consideration of the range of nursery activities, both permanent areas, such as sand and water and special resources that may be needed. There should also be some space and flexibility for spontaneous and independent learning. As Lally (1991) has stated, it is careful planning that makes spontaneous learning possible.

Medium term plans are required to ensure that there is a continuity within the learning programme and that children can progress appropriately, although the OfSTED inspection framework requires that there is priority given to: personal and social development; language and literacy and mathematics. Often medium term plans are developed around a theme or topic, such as *All about me* or *Autumn*. A topic web may be devised which outlines various experiences and activities that could take place. It is useful if boxes are assembled containing artefacts, documents, pictures, posters, and other resources relevant to each topic. A topic will group activities around a context and these activities and experiences should further the children's understanding, skills and knowledge in a systematic way. These experiences can be grouped under the *Desirable Outcomes* headings (as well as other headings eg Humanities, Technology, IT etc) to ensure that all areas have the appropriate coverage. There should also be a flexible timeframe. The Rumbold Report (1990) stresses the fact that to be successful, planning for the curriculum "involves clear perceptions about the various objectives of the curriculum and how different activities can contribute to their achievement" (para 76). The topic web or plan should, then, be clearly constructed with learning in mind and not as a set of random (brainstormed) experiences to occupy the children's time. It should also have some kind of flexibility within it to allow for spontaneous learning experiences that may arise unexpectedly or to allow for changes following observations and assessments of children's learning and development. Certain topics or themes could be used at different times of the year to focus on certain aspects of the learning programme. For example, a medium-term plan based on the theme *Nursery Rhymes* could be used to emphasise language and literacy aspects of the *Desirable Outcomes*, whilst also developing other skills and concepts. The theme or topic *All about me* could be used to enable children to explore their self-identities and others' identities and foster empathy with people from diverse backgrounds.

Short-term plans may cover specific activities and detail the aims or learning outcomes for the activities and how these link to the medium term plans. They should also include details of the grouping of the children and what the children may be expected to do as well as details of adult involvement and interaction. It can be useful to include a list of resources needed for activities with details of some of the vocabulary that should be covered. Short-term plans need to incorporate assessments made of children and can be on different levels, either for individual children, for small groups of children or for larger groups.

It has long been acknowledged that it is important for early years practitioners to work in partnership with parents. The *Desirable Outcomes* formulate a set of guidelines which state that "partnership needs to be a two-way process with opportunities for knowledge, expertise and information to flow both ways" (p.7). The guidelines establish a framework in which early years practitioners recognise the role parents and carers play in the education of their own children and the importance of information being exchanged between the nursery and home. The Rumbold Report (1990) states the importance of establishing partnerships with parents to allow for effective continuity between home and nursery for children, which will "ensure that the provision made reflects and values their cultural and language background" (p.14). *Te Whariki*, the New Zealand curriculum, also states the significance of having a multicultural heritage with "a diversity of beliefs about childrearing practices, kinship roles, obligations, codes of behaviour, and what kinds of knowledge are valuable" (p.18). It is one of the aims of *Te Whariki* that the curriculum will support cultural diversity and the identities of all children and their families and "help children gain a positive awareness of their own and other cultures" (p.18). Issues related to parent involvement are also addressed at some length in the final chapter.

Whalley (1997), has made this an important part of her early years centre at Pen Green and has negotiated a set of values in which the rights of parents and children are recognised and acknowledges that being a parent is a "complex and difficult role" (p.6). These values are translated into practice at Pen Green, which provides spaces for parents and educators from other support agencies and organisations to give help to parents who may need it. Whalley (1997) outlines some practical ways of improving partnerships, including creating a welcoming environment and encouraging parents to be involved within the setting and working with the children. At Pen Green parents have responded positively to this involvement and said that it has "boosted their own skills and brought them support, friendship, enjoyment, a better understanding of their own child and a sense of achievement" (p.27). There is now also research evidence from New Zealand to suggest that when parents are directly involved in supporting children's learning in early childhood settings there are measurable and lasting effects on the achievement of the children (Wylie, 1996). Other centres, such as Hillfields and Dorothy Gardner which we have mentioned (and many which we have not) have similarly effective parent involvement strategies, based on negotiated partnerships.

Research evaluated by Sylva and Siraj-Blatchford (1995) in Ethiopia, Indonesia, Jamaica and Egypt considers the links between home and school. The authors of this report assert the importance of involving parents and the local community in the construction and implementation of the curriculum. When they begin school or nursery, children and their parents "bring to the school a wealth of cultural, linguistic and economic experience which the school can call upon" (p.37). Sylva and Siraj-Blatchford conclude that:

"It therefore becomes the responsibility of the teacher to localise the curriculum and to enlist the support of the local community and families in framing school policy and practice and making the school and educational materials familiar and relevant to the children's experience" (p.37).

Parents need to be given information about the curriculum and learning outcomes and about the achievement of their children. Sharing information of this kind demands a shared understanding of what children are learning. Early years practitioners will need to establish a dialogue with parents that is meaningful to them. Observations of children can be mutually exchanged between staff and parents in an informal way and showing any assessments that have been done as part of the record keeping processes can be a more formal exchange of understandings. We suggest many practical ways of doing this in the last chapter. Research conducted by Sharp (1997) showed that 53% of parents valued having their views listened to and taken into account when choosing a nursery setting for their children.

Assessment and evaluation

Assessment is about understanding the learning and development of children and will affect the decisions made about the activities and experiences that may be planned with and for the children, both as a group and as individuals. Young children in the early years are diverse in their abilities, culture and experiences and assessments must reflect these diversities and be flexible enough to allow the possibilities of these variances. This being the case, evaluation and assessment must take place at different levels. Evaluation procedures should take place in the nursery so that it can be ensured that the human interactions and the learning programme provide a learning environment based on the *Desirable Outcomes*. There must also be in place a form of assessment to address the learning and development of children in the setting. The planning of the general programme in the nursery and for individual children can then be modified as a result of such evaluations and assessments. Assessment should give useful information about learning and development and can occur spontaneously or be planned to address a specific issue. Assessment that focuses on the children's learning and development should focus on individual children over a period of time and take into account the context of learning. Single observations can only provide a limited understanding and therefore a number of observations need to be built upon over a longer period of time, so that a more sophisticated understanding can be developed.

Drummond (1993) outlines three questions, which should to be asked by practitioners when they are assessing children. The first of these questions is 'what is there to see?' and this is about how to best assess children in different contexts and engaged in diverse and varied activities, both structured and unstructured play. The second question is 'how best can we understand what we see?' and this refers to the interpretations practitioners make of their observations and more formal assessments. The third question, 'how can we use the understandings gained from assessments?' is about how observations and assessments of children can be used to further their development and learning. Hutchin (1996) states the importance of the children themselves being involved in the assessment process:

"The purpose of the assessment process is to make explicit children's achievements, celebrate their achievements with them, then help them to move forward to the next goal. Without children's involvement in the assessment process assessment becomes a judgmental activity, resulting in a one-way view of a child's achievement" (p.9).

Hutchin continues by asserting that children's *significant achievement* needs to be used as an assessment tool, which will develop into a Record of Achievement for each child.

Assessment by significant achievement is based on three principles. These are: that the assessment process must include the child; assessment must enhance learning and teaching; assessment should be manageable (Clarke, 1995). What is important is that there is an "assessment dialogue" (p.13) established between adults and children which allows children to understand why they are engaging in certain activities. For this to occur, adults must plan effectively, and ensure that they are clear why children are engaging in planned activities. The adult needs to observe the children and question them about their learning, thus enabling the child to be active in their own learning and assessment. When there is an occurrence of something significant for that child a permanent record can be made. Significant achievement can be defined as "any leap in progress, something, which, from then on, will affect everything the child, does. It may be the first time a child does something.., or it may be when the teacher is sure that a particular skill or concept has now been thoroughly demonstrated" (p.14). The recording of the dialogue may be an adult written observation or a piece of work directly from the child.   The recording of significant achievement needs to take into account the context in which the achievement occurred and should include a note of why the event or piece of work was significant for that child. These annotations can then be included in a portfolio or Record of Achievement for each child.   Hutchin (1996) states that tracking   significant   achievement   consists   of   observing achievement, involving the child, making the assessment, recording the achievement and finally planning what the child needs to do next.   This clearly demonstrates the important relationship between planning and assessment procedures.

Baseline assessment

In addition to the procedures for nursery assessment processes, there may be a need for some settings to carry out baseline assessment on children. Baseline assessment is statutory for all Local   Authority   Schools   in   the   United   Kingdom   from September 1998. Local Education Authorities must ensure that schools within their area are using an accredited scheme to assess children who are entering compulsory education.   The aim of baseline assessment is to establish the skills and knowledge children have before they start their compulsory years of schooling, so that there can be some measurement of the progress they have made *during* Key Stage 1 and so that there can be a comparison with the Key Stage 1 Standard Attainment Tests (SATs). This has been termed as "Relative pupil progress" (SCAA, 1996), which will enable schools "to establish whether or not children are making the kind of progress that it is reasonable to expect given their starting point" (p.10).   This is often termed as *'value-added'*, because it is believed that the tests can show the school's contribution to each child's learning and development. Various schemes are already in operation throughout the country, but often rely on a set task for the children to do, observed and controlled by the adults in the setting.   Also, there is an emphasis on attributing a numerical score to achievement, which can then be compared with numerical scores achieved for the SATs.

There have been criticisms levelled at these kinds of assessment procedures.   Gipps and Stobart (1993), consider that such assessments have limitations in their basic design and in the way that an individual teacher may administer or deliver the test. Additionally, there may be discrepancies in the way the results for individual children are interpreted.   Different teachers may also interpret children's understanding differently.   They may also be a danger that some children will be labelled as a result of tests that are administered in this way.   In all kinds of assessment, there must be vigilance to ensure that assumptions about children are not made, especially about children who have different cultural backgrounds, or who may have English as an additional language.   Siraj-Blatchford (1994) states, "Our knowledge is not value-free, therefore our assessments need to be monitored. The best way to achieve this is to talk to other staff and consciously to evaluate the statements that we make regarding each child's progress" (p.90). Many local authorities are providing staff with training in assessment procedures and are encouraging the use of moderation across teacher assessments and schools.

Assessment and inspection
Assessment should also be made of the quality of the provision itself. Evaluation processes of this kind will identify whether the programmed curriculum and planned experiences are providing adequately for the children in the setting. It has been widely accepted that the notion of what constitutes 'quality' in early years settings is "a value laden, subjective and dynamic concept which varies with time, perspective and place" (Pascal et al, 1997, p.40). Although there is an inspection framework, enforced via Registered Nursery Inspectors by the OfSTED, this

may not be adequate to define notions of quality in early years settings. As explored in Chapter 2, the early years sector is so diverse that it may not be desirable to use the same framework for all settings within the sector. Moss, in Moss and Pence 1994, writes that the OfSTED inspection schedule is deficient because it focuses on a narrow range of experts who "control the process of definition and evaluation on the basis of technical expertise" (p.5). This creates an approach to evaluation that is exclusionary and is involved with "the exercise of power and control" (p.172). That is, the inspection framework provides a powerful way of imposing the *Desirable Outcomes* on early years settings, as inspectors must report according to their judgement as to how far the setting is likely to allow the children to achieve the *Desirable Outcomes*. The current inspection framework is used as a universal measure, with no differences countenanced for different settings. More particularly the views of people who use the setting, such as parents and children and the values of the staff who work there, are not considered to be relevant to the process of evaluation of quality. Pence and Moss, argue that what is required is a new model of evaluation based on the participation of such people and also with the "recognition of values, beliefs and interests underpinning definitions" (p.172). This will lead to specific definitions of quality which will be relevant to each setting and which will be constantly evolving and dynamic. We sympathise with this idea but would argue that it does not have to be one way or other and that both ways are needed to ensure comparability and celebrate diversity.

This is an important idea to understand. Even though settings may be judged via the OfSTED inspection framework, each setting can also be actively involved in their own evaluation according to their own explicit criteria. This type of assessment will have a number of advantages for the setting and for the children and families who use it. The appraisal values can be negotiated and made in the cultural context in which the nursery operates.   Further, any notions of quality evaluations must include strategies which promote equality.   With an inclusionary and negotiated framework social justice strategies can be furthered via a systematic approach to analysis of the early years setting, allowing practices and procedures to be devised that ensure equality is addressed for all children and their families.

Early years improvement strategies
In New Zealand, early years settings are required to develop statements on their practices and the philosophies that underpin their practice, in conjunction with users of the settings. The *Te Whariki* (1996) document refers to the principles "relating learning to the wider world and of providing the flexibility to respond to different conditions, different needs, and the expectations of local communities" (p.43).   Additionally, each early years setting is required to continually assess itself and the quality of its provision according to its own values and context. This is termed as a "continuing dialogue" (p.29) to be engaged in with the people involved in the provision and with the local community, so that it can "encourage particular challenges and activities and ...provide for the cognitive, social, emotional, and physical development of the children" (p.29).

Research can also help people involved in settings find perspectives on quality. The on-going research being conducted on the cohort of children who were involved in the Perry Pre-school Programme using a High/Scope curriculum has demonstrated the importance of allowing children to make certain decisions about their learning. Schweinhart and Weikart (1993) have continued to research the cohort of children. This group of children was chosen because they were identified as being at high risk of failing in school. The study outlines the benefits that the High/Scope Curriculum has incurred for this group, who are now twenty seven years old. These adults at twenty seven demonstrated a greater social responsibility than their peers who were not involved in any early years programme. Additionally, the High/Scope group had a higher economic status and had achieved better educationally (Barnett, 1996). A later study (Schweinhart and Weikart, 1997) has also compared children involved in the High/Scope project, a group of children who had attended an early years setting based on play and those involved in more teacher directed pre-school instruction. This study, conducted when the children were twenty three years old, demonstrated that those who had been involved in direct instruction were more likely to be involved in criminal activity as adults. Additionally, 47% of this group had been treated for emotional impairment or disturbance at some point in their educational lives, compared to only 6% of the High/Scope project and less directed early years attendees. The researchers suggest that the evidence may infer that the High/Scope project curriculum and the early years settings based on play have more positive effects on children (and consequently on the adults they become) because of the emphasis on "planning, social reasoning, and other social objectives." These aspects were absent from the settings based on more direct instruction (p.117). The researchers argue that a well-defined curriculum model should be present in the early years setting, based on child-initiated learning activities.

Pascal and Bertram (1997) have led a project on practice development to "evaluate and improve the quality and effectiveness of early learning available to 3/4-year-old children in a wide range of education and care settings" (p.40), and to compare the "quality of learning provided in a diverse range of early childhood education and care settings across the UK" (p.40). The project has identified a framework for quality organised around "dimensions of quality" (p.41). These were identified from a variety of data, including questionnaires to managers and head teachers in different early years settings. These dimensions include planning and assessment strategies as well as the curriculum itself and the relationships and interactions within the nursery. Also included are dimensions relating to equality of opportunity and partnerships with parents. Pascal and Bertram recommend that two observation techniques be used to assess the quality dimensions. The first is concerned with observing the level of a child's involvement in a particular activity or experience, and focuses on such things as the level of persistence and concentration of the child. This technique allows for the observer to pay attention to the process of learning rather than to outcomes alone. The second technique observes aspects of adult interaction with children that affect their learning. These aspects are: "sensitivity; stimulation and autonomy" (p.41). The data obtained from these observation techniques can provide some insight into the quality of the setting, and can be used to improve the provision for the children.

In order to focus on important aspects of the provision, an audit of the setting could be conducted. An audit should determine what the nursery is doing well and what things need to improve and how well the provision is working towards its aims and ethos. The Scottish Education Office (1996) recommends a self-evaluation audit using the headings: accommodation and resources; children's development and learning; effectiveness of provision and management issues. These can be useful in beginning the process of evaluation and can be prioritised so that there is not too much to do at any one time. The next step is to consider what sort of evidence is needed to further the process and who should collect this evidence. Ideally, all members of staff should be informed at every stage of the audit and involved in collecting and interpreting evidence related to the headings chosen for the evaluation. Methods of evidence collecting could involve questionnaires to parents, interviews with children and observations of various areas and the way in which the children use them. The document cited above from the Scottish Education Office uses the concept of *Performance Indicators* for the evaluation of evidence so that there can be judgements made about certain aspects of the provision.

Once the audit has been conducted, there needs to be time for reflection and analysis of the data and then decisions can be made about which aspects are working well and which aspects need to be developed further. Staff could look at a range of self-evaluation instruments for their setting such as the above or the Early Childhood Environmental Rating Scale (1998) which has recently been revised, to decide which auditing systems will be the most useful. It is also important to plan how this improvement may come about. Some consideration may be made to the list of areas outlined below. This is by no means an extensive schedule but could be used as a springboard for an audit.

Environment and basic care
Consider:
♦ if toileting routines are sensitive to children's needs
♦ whether individual nutritional needs are met
♦ whether the procedures for accidents, emergencies and illness are adequate
♦ whether all members of staff are able to deal with distressed and unsettled children
♦ whether staff establish appropriate relationships with the children and with their parents
♦ whether that all procedures for health and safety are appropriately managed and understood by all staff members
♦ whether all the rules are necessary, or are some negotiable or unnecessary

♦   whether there are effective procedures to deal with child
     abuse and whether everyone understands what their
     responsibilities are in regard to the reporting of abuse
♦   how the nursery environment reflects its aims and ethos
♦   how staff minimise the effects of their own stress on the
     children
♦   whether staffing levels allow for all the individual needs
     of the children to be met
♦   how staff are valued and supported in their own
     professional advancement

Children's learning and development
Personal and Social development
Consider:

♦   how self-help skills are encouraged and the effectiveness
     of the support given to encourage children's
     independence
♦   the flexibility of the routines and how the programme
     gives opportunities for children to make their own
     choices
♦   whether there are aspects of the environment which
     allow children to experience a sense of belonging and
     responsibility
♦   whether the planned programme allows children an
     understanding of safety issues
♦   whether the procedures for dealing with unacceptable
     behaviour are adequate and are understood by all staff
     members
♦   whether all staff are able to challenge stereotypes and
     racial abuse if they come across them
♦   how staff deal with situations where children are
     excluded by others from their play
♦   whether children engage appropriately in role play using
     collaborative strategies

Language and literacy
Consider:

- whether all staff are able to communicate effectively with the children and use appropriate vocabulary
- how children communicate with adults and with other children
- whether the programme provide for different interactions between adults and children
- how multi-lingual children and their families included in the programme
- whether the stories told, books read and symbols used in the setting reflect a wide cultural context

Mathematics
Consider:

- whether children see mathematics being used for different purposes and in different places
- whether children regularly hear and use mathematical ideas and terms in their play
- whether children work with adults using numbers in meaningful contexts
- whether children are encouraged to estimate and predict and perceive patterns

Creative development
Consider:

- whether there a wide range of creative activities and experiences for the children to engage in and the outcomes of these for the children
- how creative activities reflect a wider cultural context as well as the children's own cultural backgrounds
- whether children are able to develop an interest and ability in music and dance

♦ whether all the children are able to be involved in creative activities and experiences and spend time exploring those aspects which interest them most

Knowledge and understanding of the world
Consider:

♦ how children are supported appropriately to explore and solve problems
♦ whether staff support the children when they make mistakes and encourage learning from these errors
♦ whether there are opportunities for children to use real objects and tools
♦ whether there are genuine opportunities for children to explore the consequences of their actions
♦ how members of staff deal with children's questions about birth and death and upsetting situations.
♦ whether there are agreed procedures discussed with parents and carers

Physical development
Consider:

♦ whether there are places where children can move in a less restrained manner
♦ how the programme encourages children to develop physical control
♦ whether there are playthings and toys that are appropriate and versatile for supporting physical development
♦ whether children can combine physical activities with other areas of the curriculum such as music and language

Partnerships with parents and carers
Consider:

♦ whether the procedures used to communicate with parents and carers are effective

- whether all staff members are able to communicate appropriately
- how daily information about children is shared and whether this is adequately achieved by all members of staff
- how the nursery welcomes new children and their parents
- whether staff are able to support parents in their role as carers and educators (see final chapter)

Assessment and planning
Consider:
- whether the system for assessment provides sufficient information for all members of staff and parents and carers
- whether all members of staff contribute to the planning of the programme
- whether all members of staff implement the programme appropriately
- how does the planned programme represent the context of the nursery
- which activities and experiences are most popular and why

Once a schedule has been drawn up and the data collected, time can be taken to reflect on the results and then decisions can be taken about which areas to work on. Long-term plans can then be drafted that make reference to the evaluation and which can then be incorporated into medium term plans for the nursery programme. In this way a process of evaluation, assessment and planning can be ongoing, with each level and stage informing the other and with all staff, parents and carers and children involved.

Chapter 4

Curriculum content and practice

Language and literacy

The *Desirable Outcomes* for speaking and listening state that children should be able to:

- listen attentively
- talk about their experiences
- use increasing vocabulary to express thoughts and explore meanings
- take part in role play and make up their own stories
- use and enjoy books
- know that pictures and words have meaning and that pages turn, text reads from left to right and from top to bottom
- recognise their own names and some familiar words
- recognise letters of the alphabet by shape and sound
- associate sounds with patterns in rhymes, with syllables and with words and letters
- use pictures, symbols, familiar words and letters in their writing to communicate meaning
- write their names with appropriate use of upper and lower case letters

In the early years, there must be a focus on spoken language for a range of purposes and in a variety of contexts. The work of Vygotsky (1978) has drawn attention to children's acquisition of language in a social context and the precept that children's cognitive development is aided by language. It is through language that children are able to make discoveries and understand new experiences. The speaking and listening programme in a early years setting should allow children to learn to use language to: question and answer; plan; recall and report; formulate hypotheses; communicate with others; exchange ideas; reflect and interpret responses from others.

The research of people such as Tizard and Hughes (1984) has alerted practitioners to the rich linguistic environment children are part of outside nursery. It is the early years practitioner's task to build on skills already learned. To do this and to enable new concepts and understandings to be acquired, the early years practitioner must provide a model of talk for children and demonstrate the use of language for speculation, enquiry, exploration and debate. It is important that young children are introduced to the correct terminology to describe objects and feelings and that interactions between adults and children are of the highest quality. Browne (1996) has identified significant features of this interaction. These include: listening; summarising; orientating to significant aspects of learning; asking a limited number of genuine questions and encouraging children to talk while they are working out solutions to problems.

It is important that there is a programme for speaking and listening that allows children to practice their skills for a range of audiences and in purposeful contexts. Additionally, resources should be provided which support children's interactions with each other and allow for discussion and sharing of information. The role play area can be used as rich environment for language development and appropriate language can be encouraged in different social situations. Most activities in the nursery will offer opportunities for speaking and listening, but staff needs to focus talk and plan activities that make it necessary for children to speak and listen for different purposes.

Children who speak English as an Additional Language (EAL)

should have their first language valued and reflected in the nursery setting. Multi-lingualism is the norm in many communities across the globe and should not be viewed as a problem or deficiency. Practitioners can allow children and their families to share their knowledge of other languages, thereby fostering children's self-esteem and confidence as well as their cultural identity. It is also of benefit to monolingual children who have little insight into what it means to be bilingual or multilingual, indeed it might encourage them to see having more than one language as quite normal and therefore be more positive about their own development in this area in future schooling.

Role play café
Audience: Other children and adults
Key skills: Adapting speech to role play situation; using widening vocabulary; making decisions about how to communicate.
Activity: The role play area was changed into a café. The staff discussed with children their experiences of eating in cafés and restaurants, and menus were devised and written. When playing in the café, adults encouraged children to communicate with each other and to use language in a social context.

Describing objects
Audience: Other children
Key skills: Developing descriptive vocabulary; discussing attributes of objects.
Activity: A variety of objects were collected relating to a theme and put in a covered box. During circle time the box was presented to the children. The children were asked to close their eyes and the adults removed an object and described it. The children tried to guess what it was. Various attributes of the item were discussed and then the children were invited to

describe another object.

Extension: Objects could be hidden in various places and children could try to find them from verbal clues.

Brainstorming

Audience: Other children

Key skills: Expanding vocabulary; using language in a group to expand ideas

Activity: Using the theme*Toys*, the children were asked during circle time to tell an adult any words and feelings they can think of associated with that theme. The adult wrote these words and drew pictures onto a large sheet of paper. The adult accepted all the children's ideas and helped the children to expand their ideas.

Extension: The maps or webs could be displayed to help children with their writing.

Relay storytelling

Audience: Other children and adults

Key skills: Using language appropriate to story telling; developing an awareness of audience; listening and being receptive to other children

Activity: With a small group, an adult explained to the children that not all stories are written down and told the story of the Three Little Pigs. The adult then started another story and invited a child to continue with it. The story was then passed on to other children until it seemed to be finished.

Literacy is important in our society and fluency in reading and writing is necessary in order to participate fully in that society. Also necessary is the ability to analyse and respond to reading and writing in complex ways. As the 21st Century approaches, children will need to be able to access and evaluate information from books, from information technology sources and using a variety of other means from our information-rich society. From recent research, we now know that learning to read and write is a multi-dimensional process and that a number of strategies are required for fluency. Children need to be actively engaged in this learning and enabled to orchestrate different skills and understandings. Additionally, children must realise that reading is a purposeful activity and a communicative one.

Children entering the nursery and early years setting, may have already gained some important understandings of literacy, including knowledge of story forms and book conventions. These need to be developed through the early years literacy curriculum. Similarly, children will have been exposed to print and writing in different forms, and may have begun to make marks themselves. By making marks, children are demonstrating an ability to form symbolic representations of their experiences. Explorations of a child's own name will begin the process of actively discovering writing for themselves.

For children to engage in reading and writing they require an understanding of the process of literacy. It is important that adults who are planning literacy experiences and activities for children are clear about the audience for the writing, the form, function and purpose of the writing. Positive attitudes towards literacy should be fostered and adults in the setting need to be good role models. Young children need to see adults reading and writing and involved in routine writing in the setting. It is becoming increasingly recognised that literacy is not merely a set of skills and processes, but a tool we use to advance our thinking. Whitehead (1990) expresses it thus: "Literacy is not just a performance skill with the written system of language but a cognitive tool that transforms our capacity for self-reflection, mental re-organisation and evaluation" (p.142).

Sharing a large text

Key skills: Gaining an understanding of print conventions; how a book is held and read; the directional rules of writing (English is read from right to left and from top to bottom); print carries the same message whenever it is read; print is made up of words; words are comprised of letters; stories have a particular form and structure; reading can be engaged in for different purposes.

Activity: A large book such as *Each Peach Pear Plum* (Ahlberg and Ahlberg 1977) can be read with a small group of children. Directional conventions and rhyming words can be discussed with the children.

Extension: Shared writing can be undertaken, with the adult acting as scribe and the children as the story tellers. Focus on one or more of the print conventions to talk about whilst writing on a large piece of paper attached to an easel or flip chart. This text can then be illustrated by the children and made into a large book for sharing.

Using an information book to investigate a topic
Audience: Other children
Key skills: Reading for a different purpose (gaining information)
Activity: As part of a topic, non-fiction books can be introduced for gaining information. These books can be read instead of a story and should form part of the permanent book collection of the setting, so that children can choose these books themselves. Additionally, information books can be used as part of a display or interest table concerning a certain topic or theme
Extension: Information retrieval skills can be introduced, such as using the contents page, index, pictures and headings to find the appropriate information. Information technology can be used for information retrieval also.

Writing letters and messages

Audience: Other children and adults

Key skills: Writing for a purpose and in a certain form

Activity: This could be introduced by reading *The Jolly Postman*. A Post Office could be set up as a role play area and a visit to a post office arranged. The children could be encouraged to write to each other, to other adults in their setting and to significant adults in their lives, or to story and nursery rhyme characters. Materials and resources appropriate to this activity should be provided, including paper of differing sizes and colours and envelopes.

Extension: An adult could 'conference' individual children and discuss with them their writing and the marks they have made, talking about initial sounds and letters where appropriate.

Mathematics

The *Desirable Outcomes* for mathematics state that children should be able to:

- use mathematical language to describe shape, position, size or quantity
- recognise and recreate mathematical patterns
- compare, sort, match, order, sequence and count using every day objects
- be familiar with counting games, number rhymes, songs and stories
- recognise and use numbers to 10
- through practical activities, begin to solve problems, record numbers and show an awareness of number operations

Mathematics is concerned with patterns and uses a special language with terms whose meanings often differ from every day definitions. Children need to be exposed to this mathematical language throughout their day and in conjunction with real experiences and meaningful activity. Tidying up, for example, is a mathematical activity, as it involves sorting, ordering and classifying objects. Discussion can take place about where objects belong and why. Considering whether all the bricks will fit into a particular box or which container will hold more beads are examples of problem-solving situations which use the mathematical concepts of volume, size and shape. Similarly, when children are having their tea or morning drink, adults can talk about how many cups are needed and question what would happen if one child was not having a drink that morning, and so introduce number operations in a practical situation. The role play area can be a rich source for engaging in mathematical problem solving. Arranging the role play area as a shop, for example, will give children experience of prices and using money in a familiar context. In a home corner role play area there can be opportunities to talk about numbers such as telephone numbers, calendars and diaries, and experiences of sorting and matching cutlery and crockery can be gained.

Mathematics is often abstract and disembedded from any context and as adults we can find mathematical meanings difficult to comprehend. Sometimes, our own negative experiences of mathematical learning at school remain with us and lead to a belief in our own inability. However, our own negativity towards mathematics and numeracy can be made positive. By helping young children to perceive mathematical concepts and solve problems, we can ourselves reach a better understanding of mathematics. Recent research has suggested that imaging is important in the understanding of mathematics.

This is about perceiving patterns and visualising sequences.
It is very important to use correct terminology and language when talking to children about mathematical ideas and concepts, and every opportunity should be made to talk about these. Numbers, shapes, patterns and measurements are all around the children and they should form part of the every day conversations we have with children. Whilst it is important that

adults in the setting take full advantage of spontaneous situations to discuss numbers and mathematical concepts, it is also important that there are planned activities which introduce some ideas and provide extension activities for the more able children.

Clapping rhythm
Key skills: Recognising and reproducing patterns
Activity: Ask the children to copy a short and simple clapping rhythm, e.g. *clap, clap, clap.* Then introduce a *silence, clap, silence, clap.* The children can make up their own simple clapping rhythms for others to copy. So that the rhythms can be reproduced, symbols or numbers can then be written.
Extension: Introduce and devise more complex rhythms, which require children to count the number of claps they need to reproduce. Music has a strong mathematical content and the basis for understanding rhythm is mathematical.

Using a number line
Key skills: Ordering, comparing and sequencing numbers; recognition of numbers; developing an awareness of conservation of number
Activity: Look at the numbers 1-10 on a number line and match these to real objects, such as beads or blocks. Have one bead next to the number 1, two beads next to the number 2 and so on. Discuss with the children which number has the most beads next to it and which the fewest. There can also be a discussion of how the numbers are written in other community languages and consideration of the differences between the scripts.
Extension: An awareness of number operations, such as simple addition and subtraction can be discussed.

Dice game
Key skills: Counting skills; understanding of the concepts of

more than and fewer than; recognising patterns in sets.

Activity: In a large space, or outside, have a group of children standing on a line drawn on the floor. The children throw large dice and take as many steps as shown on the dice. The game can finish when a child reaches an agreed finishing point.

Extension: This activity can lead to discussions on length. Additionally some children may wish to discuss the fact that this game is unfair because the participants may be using different size steps. This could lead to consideration of measures and measuring activities. Children could also be invited to look at different arrangements of dots for the numbers one to six, to encourage conservation of number concepts.

Knowledge and understanding of the world
The desirable outcomes in this area encompass a number of different skills and can be broken down further into concepts associated with the disciplines of history, geography, science and design and technology.

Scientific concepts

- explore features of living things, natural and made objects
- look closely at similarities, differences, patterns and change
- talk about and sometimes record their observations
- question why things happen and how things work

The Rumbold Report (1990) states that for young children "the world of science and technology is inescapable" (para. 55) and acknowledges that learning scientific ideas in the early years will involve, mostly, discussing with children their observations and descriptions of every day events and experiences. Once again, the use of accurate terminology will be important and adults must ensure that they are using the appropriate language.

Scientific investigation involves questioning, formulating ideas or hypotheses, experimenting, observing and communicating findings. In order for this process to be possible, children must be able to describe objects and classify them according to their attributes and be able to sort objects by the features they have in common. Sorting activities, such as tidying up, can be discussed with the children in terms of things that are the same and things that are different about certain objects so that children will begin to perceive relationships between things.

Popcorn

Children can engage in scientific activity during cooking times. Here, children can use all their senses to observe changes in state of substances.

Key skills: Investigating changes; observing, questioning and hypothesising; communicating observations

Activity: A small group of children observed raw popcorn. The adult helped the children to describe the corn, using words such as hard and shiny. They also discussed how the corn may have grown. The children were invited to suggest what might happen to the corn kernels once they became hot. The adult then put the corn in a pan over the heat and waited for the corn to pop. As the corn was popping, the children were helped to describe the sounds they could hear and question why it might make this noise. Once the corn had finished popping and cooled, the children were shown the corn. Again, they were encouraged to describe the corn and think about the changes that had occurred during the heating process. During circle time, some of the children reported to the other children what they had observed during the activity. The adults had taken photographs of the corn before and after cooking and these were put into a recipe book with other recipes from cooking activities.

Slopes

Key skills: observing; predicting events; hypothesising; using equipment appropriately and safely; reporting findings to others
Activity: In the outside play area, a group of children had been observed by the adult talking about how the bicycles went faster down the sloped part of the area than on the flat surface. The adult went inside and fetched some toy cars and some wooden ramps from the construction kit. The children were then invited to run the cars down the ramps and to think how they could make the cars run faster. One child suggested raising the ramp so that the slope was steeper. This was tried out and compared with a less steep ramp. The children were asked to consider why this might be. The children thought that the steeper the slope, the faster the car would run down. During circle time the children were invited to tell the rest of the group what they had found out.

Historical concepts
  • talk about their families and past and present events in their lives

In order to engage in talk about the past and present, children need to be introduced to the concepts of time and change that occurs during time periods. Time is a difficult concept for children to grasp and there are two aspects to learning about time. One is gaining an understanding of time intervals and the other is the passage of time such as the change of the seasons and the time on a clock. These can occur as part of every day activity of the nursery. During circle time, the children can be asked what day of the week it is and how they know. The children may know that it is a certain day because certain activities or events occur on particular days, or they may have remembered what day it was the day before. This particular aspect is about sequencing events in time, and can be developed by describing past events and anticipating and planning for future events.

Preparing for an outing

Key skills: Describing past events; anticipating and planning for future events.

Activity: Before going on an outing, the children can be prepared by being asked to remember the last time they went on an outing with the nursery and to think about what they needed to take with them and what to do to keep safe. They can then help to plan the outing and prepare for it by discussing significant details with adults.

Family time line

Key skills: Understanding of concept of old and young, describing different aspects of families; distinguishing differences and similarities among individuals and families.

Activity: Children can be invited to draw pictures of members of their family or household on a time line from the youngest member to the oldest member. This activity can initiate talk about different languages that are spoken and home and how to say and write the words for mother, father, sister, brother, and so on, in different languages. This activity could also be extended to consideration of special babies within different religions, such as Jesus, Krishna, Guru Nanak, Moses.

Geographical concepts

- talk about where they live, their environment and the purpose of some of its features

Geography is about people and places and the interaction between them. For young children, the emphasis will be on helping to make sense of the world around them, both the physical environment (weather, land forms, vegetation) and the human environment (transport, settlements, industries, employment).

Developing geographical vocabulary is important in the early years. Spatial words such as up, right, behind, can be developed through physical activities. Physical features of places can be discussed during story sessions, or information books can be used to develop one theme, such as weather. Children can also be involved in planning the nursery environment, such as the layout of furniture and outdoor equipment. This will involve discussion of geographical issues, such as likes and dislikes of their environment.

Role play area - travel agent
Key skills: Looking at maps and globes; understanding how journeys may be undertaken; comparing different places with the local environment
Activity: A travel agent was set up in the role play area. This involved the children in looking at travel brochures, comparing hot and cold places and then relating these to a globe and world maps. The adults helped the children to make their own passports and there were related activities planned, such as packing suitcases for different climates. Information books were used to discover different things about certain other countries and these were compared with the local environment. The travel agent role play area also led to discussions about how journeys are made and a graph was drawn up showing how the children travelled to the nursery.

Field work - an outing to a City farm
Key skills: Relating knowledge and understanding to real places and people; mapping and planning; developing knowledge of employment and occupations.
Activity: There was an outing to a farm in an inner City planned. One member of staff went to visit the farm before the planned outing and collected information, including a simple map of the farm showing where various animal pens were. This map was enlarged on a photocopier and some small copies were

also made for the children to take with them. Before the visit, the children were involved in looking at the map and planning a route around the farm. This route was drawn on the large map. Once at the farm, the children could follow the route on their own maps. Members of staff at the farm also talked to the children about their work and the things they had to do to keep the animals safe and healthy. Once the children were back at the nursery, information books were used to consider other farm animals and arable farms and their function in providing food for shops and supermarkets. It was decided that an outing to a supermarket would be planned so that the children could see the produce for sale and make links with their work on farms.

Design and technology concepts

- explore and select materials and equipment to use skills such as cutting, joining, folding and building for a variety of purposes
- make appropriate use of technology to support their learning

Engaging in design and technology involves certain craft skills, using tools such as scissors, files, drills, saws and rulers and in understanding materials and structures so that problems can be solved. For early years children, having practice in using tools is crucial to developing skills. Construction kits need to be made available for young children for the learning of these skills and for discussion of health and safety issues. These kits should contain real tools scaled down for young children and a work bench should be provided with various materials for children to practice their skills. Both adults and children can often perceive technology as a gendered activity. Early years practitioners often note that girls do not freely choose technology or construction activities as much as boys. This may be because of a "capability gap" (Brown, 1993) between boys and girls. This refers to the possibility that some girls may not have had exposure to construction tools and toys and may therefore lack the skills to engage purposefully in activities in the nursery. This needs to be actively addressed by female staff giving positive role models to children and by making sure that all children are taught the appropriate skills and given encouragement to practice them.

Computers can be useful tools for young children, although John Siraj-Blatchford (in Siraj-Blatchford, 1998) makes the point that young children will not benefit from using the computer "until they have learnt to classify in at least two dimensions and deal logically with equivalence and conservation" (p.117). However, Siraj-Blatchford also alerts practitioners to the evidence which suggests that when engaged in computer activities interactions are of a high quality, "especially with regard to co-operative behaviour" (p.116).

Using the computer
Key skills: Identifying physical components of the computer; use of the mouse; identifing some commonly used keys on the keyboard
Activity: When the children are engaged in a computer program activity the adult can talk to the children about the names of the various computer components, with correct terminology, such as keyboard, mouse, monitor, disk drive and printer. The children can also be engaged in identifying some common keys, such as ENTER and some letters and numbers. During a general discussion, a set of rules could be created on computer care, for example not eating or drinking by the computer and pressing the keys gently.

Making a rag book
Key skills: Designing; joining skills

Activity: As part of the theme *Me and my family* it was decided that the children would make books for younger children. A young child's rag book was brought in to show the children and an adult cut pieces of calico into the same size and shape. The children then set about creating pictures, prints and patterns to put into the rag book. The children could then choose various methods of attaching these pictures to the book. Some pictures had a hole punched in them and were tied to the book with string or ribbon. Others glued pieces of velcro to their pictures and to the book. Some of the more able children sewed some pieces of fabric they had found into the book. This activity also gave rise to a discussion on different kinds of fastenings the children have on clothes.

Creative development
The *Desirable Outcomes* for creative development state that children should be able to:
- explore sound
- explore colour, texture, shape, space and form in two and three dimensions
- respond in a variety of ways to what they see, hear, smell, touch and feel
- show increasing ability to listen, observe and use imagination through art, music, dance, stories and imaginative play
- use a widening range of materials, suitable tools, musical instruments and other resources to express ideas and to communicate feelings

Creativity is about representing experiences, feelings and emotions. In order to do this, young children need to learn skills and to develop understandings. It has also been argued that creative development, and especially the growth of visual representation, is important for cognitive development and other

"other representational modes, for example, language acquisition and mathematical understanding" (Matthews in Blenkin and Kelly, 1996, p.150). This has also been the basis of the emphasis on representation in the nurseries in Reggio Emilia, where teachers have high expectations of the children's abilities to express their thoughts, feelings and observations in painting, drawing or other graphic ways. As in other parts of the curriculum, young children learn through meaningful activities that integrate other subject areas, such as mathematics when considering ideas of pattern. It is also important that young children develop understandings of integrating different forms including words, gestures, paintings, drawing, sculpture, building, music, dance and role play.

The *Desirable Outcomes* recognise that a multi-sensory approach is required when experiences are been expressed and represented. At the early stages of development, young children begin to scribble and build up a repertoire of scribble movements and forms. As physical skills grow more controlled these forms become more organised and representative of the world the children observe. Similarly, children will experience musical concepts, such as rhythm, in their every day lives and assimilate these. It is the early years practitioner's task to initiate and support children's responses to these daily events. Morgan (1988) outlines four areas of experiences for creative work. These are: responses to 'infinity' (for example dreams, legends, stories); responses to the environment; responses to other people and living things; responses to emotions and feelings. In order that these responses can occur, children must be skilled in using tools and practised in using different media.

For the visual arts, a nursery should ensure that children have balanced experiences, comprising colour, pattern, texture, form in two and three dimensions, drawing, and designing. Children should also have the opportunity to respond to artefacts such as paintings and sculptures from different cultures and discuss their likes and dislikes.

Windows
Key skills: Exploring space and shape in three dimensions
Activity: During a repainting of the wooden frame used for the home corner, the adults thought that the curtains needed replacing. They decided to involve the children in designing some new curtains using fabric dyes and fabric crayons. This activity led to a discussion on windows and during their next outing to the library, the children looked at different shapes and sizes of windows. They also looked at some stained glass in a church window. Back in the nursery, the children created their own windows. Some painted the colours they had seen on the stained glass, and were helped to mix the colours they wanted. Others made a collage using cellophane and fabrics. Once they were finished, they were displayed as part of a collaborative display on windows.

Musical outcomes will be accomplished by the children exploring their own voices and other instruments to become aware of the elements of music. These elements are:

- rhythm (understanding of beat and pulse)
- pitch (awareness of high/low and the effects created)
- timbre (understanding of distinctive characteristics and qualities of sound in music)
- dynamics (understanding of soft/loud and the effects created both in music and other sounds)

Children should also be introduced to patterns in sound, which will link to mathematical activities and begin to compose and create their own musical patterns to express their feelings. They can also listen to music created by others and discuss their reactions to the music.

Exploring rhythm
Key skills: Developing a sense of pulse and beat; linking physical movement to rhythm.
Activity: A group of children stand in circle with the adult and sing a nursery rhyme or song known to all the children. The children can clap to the beat, then march on the spot. Once the beat has been established by all the children, they can all walk in the circle, holding hands whilst singing the song. Each step will be taken on the beat. The children can experiment with singing in different tempos and match the speed of their steps to their singing.

Creating musical patterns
Key skills: Developing an awareness of sequences and patterns in music; compose own sequences
Activity: During a music session, a group of children were asked by the adult to copy a simple clapping rhythm. Once this had been achieved a number of times, a child was asked to create his own pattern to be followed by the other children. At a follow up session, the adult introduced another sound to the clap sequence, which was a pat on the knees. This allowed a more complex pattern to be developed. Once the children had understood this and begun to successfully create their own two sound patterns, the adult showed them cards with pictures on them. Some had a picture of hands clapping and this represented one clap. Other cards had a picture of hands with the palms facing downwards, which represented one pat. When the children had created their sequences, they were asked to arrange the cards in that sequence with the number of claps and pats represented by the number of cards used. This then made it easier for the sequence to be repeated by others, as they could follow the cards. Later the children used percussion instruments and pictures of these were used to represent sequences.

Listening to music
Key skills: Gaining an understanding of the way music can be used to express feelings and experiences; develop vocabulary to discuss music
Activity: During a session in the nursery, an adult had observed a few of the children singing some music that accompanied a television advertisement. She talked to the children about the tune and others they knew. The next day, she brought in a tape with short extracts of various types of music on and discussed with the children how these made them feel.

Physical development
The *Desirable Outcomes* for physical development state that children should be able to:
- move confidently and imaginatively, with increasing control, co-ordination and an awareness of space and of others
- use a range of large and small equipment with increasing skill
- use balancing and climbing apparatus with increasing skill
- handle appropriate tools, objects, construction and malleable materials safely and with increasing control

Physical movement is vital for children's overall learning and development and occurs during specifically planned activities as well as incidentally in the nursery. However, physical skills need to be learned by children in the early years settings, as much as intellectual skills and concepts and adults in the early years play an essential role in developing these. As Boorman writes (in Blenkin and Kelly, 1996) "Each child does need the widest possible range of movement experiences...A varied and imaginative movement programme can promote enjoyment and satisfaction in vigorous movements of the body" (p.231). As well as learning control in a range of physical movements, children will also learn to interact and negotiate with other children. Physical skills and concepts, for example in a dance medium, will also enhance the imagination and develop musical concepts and understandings.

Young children require both free play opportunities to develop their fine and gross motor skills and gain muscle tone and more structured learning activities for specific skills. For these experiences to occur, there needs to be a structured approach to planning for physical development in the setting and staff will need to be confident in the teaching of games and movement skills in order to intervene appropriately in children's activities. When considering experiences for physical development it is important to think about safety as well as providing a stimulating and challenging environment for children, with a variety of both large and small equipment. Small apparatus, such as quoits, balls, hoops, ropes and bean bags can enable skills such as rolling, bouncing, catching and throwing to be introduced and developed. These skills can then be combined into small group games. Playing games requires certain specific skills, such as throwing and catching, as well as the ability to negotiate and co-operate with others. The development of movement and dance is based on four areas: body; space; quality; relationship and experiences should be planned to advance these areas.

Movement and dance: The Sea
Key skills: Moving in rhythm; controlled movement; use of imagination; collaboration with other children
Activity: Following an outing to the seaside, a group of children were observed engaging in role play that reflected their experiences paddling in the sea. An adult worked with these children, discussing sounds associated with the sea and

movements that the waves had made. The children suggested rolling movements to imitate the waves. In order to do this, the children had to synchronise their movements. Some other children joined in pretending to paddle and splash in the sea. The adult helped to organise a short dance involving some of these movements, combined with an extract from La Mer by Debussy. This was practised and then performed to other nursery children, staff and parents.

Jumping
Key skills: Awareness of space; qualities of fast and slow
Activity: Some children had found it difficult to jump during an action song. It was decided that jumping could become a movement theme for a short period of time. A group of children were taken into the hall and each child sat in a hoop, so that they had some space around them. An adult showed the children how to jump on the spot, in the hoop, with feet together and knees bent. Once the children had practised this, a drum was introduced to set a beat. This was varied from slow to fast and the children practised jumping in time, varying the quality in that way. In a second session, the children jumped from one leg and landed on another out of the hoop and then back in. Over a number of short sessions, the children developed a repertoire of jumping movements, which they were able to use in their outside play as well as during action songs.

Using bean bags
Key skills: Throwing and catching. Playing simple games.
Activity: An adult with a small group, who had previously been introduced to throwing bean bags, demonstrated how to catch. The children were helped to stand correctly with their hands in front of their body and their fingers spread and reminded to watch the bean bag into their hands and then to pull back their hands securely into their body. The adult threw to each child a

couple of times as they stood in a circle and then organised the
children into pairs to practise both throwing and catching. At
another session, a game was played with small groups of
children using bean bags.

Personal and social development
The *Desirable Outcomes* for personal and social development
state that children should:

- have confidence and self respect
- behave in appropriate ways
- be aware of right and wrong
- work well in groups and take turns and share fairly
- treat living things, property and their environment with
  care and concern
- have good relationships with and sensitivity to others,
  including those of different cultures and beliefs
- show a range of feelings, such as wonder, joy or sorrow
- respond to cultural and religious events
- concentrate and persevere
- take initiative
- select an activity or resource
- work well independently
- have personal independence

These outcomes are concerned with the growth of awareness
and self-knowledge, as well as the development of
understandings about others. Blenkin and Whitehead, (1996)
highlight the way that play and play experiences that are
planned and of a high quality can develop these awareness
through "rehearsal". This means that children can "try out a
range of roles" and thus "practise a range of feelings such as
helplessness and power, misery and vindictiveness" (p.34).
Through play, children can also be helped with the development
of their self-esteem and learn not to be frightened by challenges
where non-achievement is a possibility. An ethos of supporting
the process of children's efforts as well as the end products will

also foster self-esteem

In the anti-bias curriculum (Derman-Sparks, 1989) four goals are identified as being necessary for young children to reach. These are: the construction of a knowledgeable, confident self-identity; comfortable, empathetic interactions with people from diverse backgrounds; critical thinking about bias; the ability to stand up for herself or himself and for others in the face of bias. These goals can be reached through the implementation of specific activities and experiences and by engaging children in discussions about social justice issues.

Appropriate behaviour can be encouraged through interactions with adults and through routines such as sharing and turn-taking. Moral and ethical issues can be discussed with children and some stories are useful for raising these matters. Through stories, children can have the opportunity to discuss their feelings and develop ideas of fairness and justice. Other early years setting routines, such as tidying up, can help children to contribute to caring for their environment. Children can be involved in making decisions about where equipment should be stored and how the outside play area could be arranged.

Outside environment
The outside play area was identified by a nursery setting as in need of work. One of the educators decided to make this her own project and was given a small budget by the management committee. She asked small groups of children about their views and together they constructed a drawing of what the outside play area might look like. The children were keen to have the wall painted with trees and butterflies and wanted to be able to plant bulbs. Although some of the ideas were modified, most of them were implemented and over the course of a year bulbs were planted and the wall was painted, using some of the

designs from the children.

The role of adults

Learning also has an important social dimension and children need to develop skills of collaboration and negotiation. Experiences and activities need to be planned that provide opportunities for children to investigate in groups and work together on discovering solutions to problems. These experiences should also challenge stereotypical views on gender, race and class and value diversity as an enriching aspect of the social environment. The adults in the early years setting are part of this social environment and the relationships that these adults establish with the children will influence the children's relationships with both adults and children in the setting. Katz (1995) has written about the importance of the establishing of an accepting and understanding relationship between adults and children in early childhood settings. This relationship will then extend to other children and be manifested in collaborative activities. These aspects are also important to be emphasised for the development of an environment and a curriculum that has an ethos of racial equality and social justice. As Siraj-Blatchford (1994) has expressed it, "Children can work and play together to share ideas, tackle problems together, and serve as role models for a culturally diverse community" (p.74). By observing and talking with children, staff in the early years setting can discover what ideas children have about diversity. These responses can then be directed toward activities and experiences for the children. The environment and the images in the nursery setting should reflect diverse abilities and current racial, ethnic, gender and economic diversity in society as a whole. Events and activities in the nursery can allow the children to develop a sense of order. Particular events can be recognised, such as cultural festivals and special days such as birthdays will enable children to understand the importance of rituals.

Skills of independence are developed by design and involve four steps: showing children how; providing practice; having children structure activities and children using the activities independently. There is involved here a transfer of decision making from the adult to the child as appropriate to each child's capabilities. This transfer is important to help children understand how their efforts can affect their learning. This control of the learning task helps children acquire motivation to continue learning.

Children also need to be helped to be independent in their physical routines, such as dressing and hygiene and also in their learning. Encouraging children to gain independence is concerned with developing attitudes, values, knowledge and skills needed to make responsible decisions. These are fostered by creating the opportunities and experiences that encourage children's motivation, curiosity, self confidence, self-reliance and a positive self-concept. This will be a lifelong process that allows children to begin to formulate their own understandings and meanings. These attitudes and values could be characterised as being about *citizenship* and are concerned with what is valued in society. Early years practitioners should help children to develop the necessary skills, understandings and attitudes to participate fully in society. Additionally, practitioners in the early years can be instrumental in fostering this process in a number of ways. Firstly, children can be encouraged to take appropriate responsibility for decision making in the early years setting. At the Dorothy Gardner Centre Nursery in London, it was decided to reorganise the nursery in response to children's perceptions about their environment. Some of the children had asked "if perhaps one or two tables and spaces might be left for their own projects and intentions" (Makins, 1997, p.87). Secondly, the learning environment itself can be supportive of children's own efforts with relevant planned experiences and activities. Thirdly, adults in the early years setting need to model appropriate behaviour and to share with children what is being done and communicate why an activity is useful. This will allow children to eventually make their own decisions, connect what they already know with what they are learning and apply new ideas. This modelling can be achieved by adults thinking aloud and talking through activities and problem-solving experiences.

Adults in the early years setting need to know the children well in order that experiences are appropriately planned for each child in the setting. It is necessary, therefore that adults observe and reflect upon the children's learning processes. There is also a need to anticipate difficulties the child may have and offer support at appropriate times. Adults need to develop a good understanding of the children's abilities, health and cultural backgrounds so that appropriate learning experiences can be planned. Although independent learning is the aim, this does not occur in isolation, but includes co-operative, small group and larger group learning. By experiencing different social groupings, children will be better able to select from a variety of settings, resources and styles that meet their needs and interests.

Adapting activities
Children come into the nursery with significant differences in their cultural backgrounds, aptitudes, interests, abilities and achievement levels and this diversity is to be valued. Activities and experiences need to be have an adaptive dimension so that all children can have access to the learning programmes of the setting. By planning activities, and more specifically through the planning of strategies to promote the learning of particular skills and concepts and the arrangement of the learning environment, this accommodation can be made. Grouping arrangements for the children also needs to be flexible so that

children can be involved in large and small group activities. Additionally, there need to be times when children can explore and learn as individuals.

The adaptive dimension always starts with the learner and adults must know what types of learning tasks are appropriate for different levels of children's cognitive, social and emotional and cultural development. Some children may need considerable support to reach the *Desirable Outcomes* and may require activities that take them step by step towards the outcomes. These *stepping stones* should be planned individually for each child according to their assessed needs. However some ideas for these are outlined below.

Personal and social development:
Creating a predictable environment and building positive relationships with children are important steps in encouraging independence in young children. Adults in the early years setting should accept young children's emotional outbursts, but also help children to express and resolve these in more positive ways. Help in articulating conflict may also aid positive resolution. A regular pattern for the day will enable children to feel secure and will also contextualise their learning. New elements and features can then be introduced gradually. Adults should work at minimising opportunities for frustrations to occur by showing genuine respect for children and applying consistent expectations for behaviour. Additionally, the environment and organisation of the setting can be instrumental in lessening opportunities for inappropriate behaviour.

Adults demonstrating respect for children and other adults in the setting can support social skills. Children can be encouraged to take care of others and adults can actively support social interactions, both through spontaneous play events and through planned social occurrences.

Language skills:
Agreed key words can be introduced as part of the every day routine, so that new vocabulary is used in a meaningful context. Talk about family members and features of the environment alongside brief outings in the locality can provide a context for talk. A widening experience can be provided through playthings, books and pictures. Conversations can be initiated with children that confirm and strengthen their self-identity and that give children time to respond appropriately. Children require good models of conversation and adults in the setting can provide this.

Labels in the nursery will reinforce the use of writing and enhance reading opportunities. Children's own names are an important tool for establishing early literacy and there should be opportunities for children to see their own name written and should be supported in attempting to write their own names.

Mathematics:
In the early stages of mathematical learning, vocabulary development is crucial to support later understanding of mathematical concepts. Numbers need to be used in every day conversation and in different contexts so that vocabulary such as 'more than', 'fewer than', 'big' and 'small' can be repeated frequently. Positional language is also important to introduce and can be used in connection with physical activities and games. The understanding of patterns provides important early mathematical experiences and play that establishes these ideas should be encouraged.

Knowledge and understanding of the world:
The opportunity to collect, sort and organise the environment is important in the establishing of early scientific concepts. This

can be achieved through every day routines such as tidying away or re-organising aspects of the learning environment. Establishing a sense of order is important and having control over certain parts of the nursery will enhance children's capacities for learning. Predicting what will happen is also a significant step in founding these concepts and ideas. Similarly, the vocabulary of estimation needs to be developed. Children need to have experience of thinking and talking about what they are doing, and adults in the setting should model this. Adults can also encourage the exploration of materials, both in two and three dimensions and raise questions with children about what they are doing. Curiosity should be encouraged in order to allow for the sustaining of interest in activities.

Creative development:
Providing a wide range of materials and tools will facilitate the development of skills associated with creativity. Young children also require opportunities to experiment with these materials and with musical instruments in their own way and experience them through all of their senses. Fantasy play and make-believe will enhance the imaginative aspects of development.

Physical development:
The programme planned for the nursery should include opportunities for young children to move their whole bodies and participate in dance experiences. There should be a balance between activities that develop fine and gross motor skills and care should be taken in ensuring that experiences offer varying degrees of challenge for children. Support can be offered but sensitively, so that children feel secure in taking risks and can accept their own abilities and limitations.

Chapter 5

Cross-curricular issues

Developing a sense of belonging

The Next Steps document clearly outlines the way the *Desirable Outcomes* flow into the requirements of Key Stage One of the National Curriculum. As such it is clearly indicated that the *Desirable Outcomes* are to be preparation for life at school. However, the aims for early education should be viewed in a wider context. The Warnock Committee Report (1978) stated aims for education thus: "To enlarge a child's knowledge, experience and imaginative understanding, and thus his awareness of moral values and capacity for enjoyment; and... to enable him (and her) to enter the world after formal education is over as an active participant in society and a responsible contributor to it." Although this report was specifically addressed to the education of children with special educational needs, this paragraph is quoted in the Rumbold Report (1990) and is an important statement for all phases of education. Early education should not, therefore, be regarded merely as a preparation for school. When planning for learning and development in an early years setting, experiences and activities should be recognised as being important in themselves and in order to equip children with necessary skills, understandings and attitudes for later learning and for life. The early years curriculum should allow children to participate and achieve in the entire education system.

As part of the planned programme for personal and social development, young children will be learning skills of independence and co-operation. These skills and attitudes will be important for children moving into school, as self-care skills are valued by teachers who may have large numbers of children in their classes. Children entering school will be expected to be able to take their own meals, so skills associated with eating are important. Equally important, however, are issues surrounding understanding healthy foods and appropriate foods within their own culture. Children who may not eat certain foods because of religious, cultural or other family practices should be able to make their needs known to adults in school and should expect to have these practices respected. Children should also have some understanding of others that may not share their own practices and preferences. Young children entering school should also have gained some strategies for gaining control of their own emotions, but also have some understanding about keeping themselves safe and be able to articulate concerns they may have.

The early years setting can encourage children to understand and have knowledge of the wider community in which they and their schools and nurseries are operating and children should be given opportunities to take some responsibility for caring for their own environment. These aspects of living in a community will be important once children are at school. In order to feel a sense of belonging in their new school setting, children will have to make new friends. Doing this requires good self-esteem and confidence. These are fostered indirectly, however there are certain skills involved in social interaction, such as having strategies to open conversation and keep them going. These can be learned and practised in the early years setting. In order for children to be a part of a school community, they will have to have an understanding of rules as well as a concept of fairness and why it is important to keep to certain modes of behaviour in particular places. Values such as reliability, honesty and courtesy will also be important to foster for children's sense of belonging. At the same time children should be positive about their own gender and ethnicity and about the opposite gender and about other ethnic groups and respect children who may be different in some way.   Skills to identify and challenge bias, prejudice and negative stereotyping can be nurtured.

Language skills will be crucial to children when they enter school, as assessments and judgements will be made according to linguistic abilities.   The early years setting programme should plan to provide children with language skills for a range of purposes and allow children to develop vocabulary in order to be expressive and supportive in their speech.   Additionally, a programme which allows children to have access to many different books and in which adults regularly talk to children about books and stories will give children important early concepts about print and literacy.   Similarly, early mathematical experiences will be important for fostering positive attitudes towards numeracy and mathematical concepts.   Having secure understandings about the use of numbers and mathematical patterns in every day life will give young children a secure awareness of the purpose of mathematics.

In addition to expressing themselves in speech, young children need to be able to express themselves creatively and imaginatively using other media such as music, dance and art. For children to fully participate in the creative life of their school, they will need to have acquired a range of techniques for articulating themselves and a repertoire of expressive body movements acquired through physical activities and through role-play experiences.   Imagination and creativity is not only important for art and design activities, but is also important in problem solving and applying new ideas to old knowledge and perceiving connections in thinking.   Additionally, thinking imaginatively will allow for innovation and experimentation, both of which are important for scientific pursuits.   Young children should be given opportunities to explore certain aspects of their physical world and be able to describe some basic properties of their immediate surroundings and should have gained some understanding of the way things change over time and the impact of their own actions on their environment.

Whilst this may give some general overview of how the early years curriculum can contribute to the National Curriculum, the remaining part of this chapter considers other learning outcomes which can be combined into an early years curriculum, taking a wider view of what it is important for young children to learn.

Values and dispositions
The New Zealand early years curriculum, *Te Whariki*, (1996) refers to the development of "dispositions" (p.44) in children. These dispositions are defined as "habits of mind" and "patterns of learning" (p.44). These will provide a framework for future independent learning and combine knowledge, skills, understandings and attitudes. The notion of independent learning links the demands of the curriculum (whether it is the National Curriculum or the *Desirable Outcomes)* with the needs of society as a whole. Once children have developed some dispositions towards learning, they can then construct 'working theories'. These are frameworks of related ideas that help children to make sense of the world and exercise some control over what happens to them. These working theories will also enable the children to begin the process of problem solving and investigation. In the early years environment these working theories can be encouraged through children participating in experiences in an active way, with their senses engaged. Children can also gain valuable understanding by observing and listening and these skills can also be supported. At the basis of the Reggio Emilia curriculum is the idea of children representing their experiences using a wide variety of techniques. The Reggio Emilia philosophy is that children have multiple ways of looking at the world and of solving the problems they find in it. To express these understandings

children use different ways or 'languages' (see Edwards et al, 1993). These languages may include the written and spoken word or media such as clay, collage, drawing, music, dance or dramatic play. The work of children in the Reggio Emilia nurseries is displayed and accompanied by photographs of the work in progress, anecdotes and transcriptions of any discussions the children may have had while they were working on the piece. This is called documentation and is a tool for children, nursery staff and parents alike to use for reflection on progress and as some indication of what the next stage of development and learning may be. It is crucial that children are able to engage in a large variety of representation techniques so that they can begin to make meaning from their experiences and gain control over their environment and take responsibility for their actions.

Whilst in society many values are implicit, there are many that can be incorporated into educational programmes. As educators and carers of young children, adults in a early years setting must decide which values they will combine into their own programme. These should be decided in consultation with parents and carers and other members of the community and should be explicitly stated as part of the ethos and philosophy of the setting. This ethos will then be the basis for the planning of the curriculum programme. Some general cross-curricular themes are considered below with suggestions for implementation.

Racial equality and inclusive practice
Starting points:
In order for children to be active and energetic thinkers they need :
- to establish a sense of trust and identity
- to develop a sense of empowerment

- to know that their home language/s are valued and supported
- to realise that their home language/s can continue to be the vehicle for learning
- to establish gender identity
- to develop an appreciation of diversity among people
- to have opportunities for meaningful play

The early childhood practices that work for minority ethnic children are the ones that work for all children. Children need the kind of early childhood experiences, in a language they understand, that turn them into enthusiastic and independent learners. They also need experiences that build on the racial, cultural and linguistic resources they bring with them to the programme (adapted from Wong-Fillmore 1991). There is a need to apply celebration and diversity of language and culture, recognising that not all cultural and language groups have equal access to the power and that simply knowing each others' differences is not enough to erase inequality (Siraj-Blatchford, 1992). First language acquisition and cognitive development are active constructive processes whereby children generate their knowledge of the world and their linguistic knowledge within a matrix of social interaction (Wells 1986).

It is important to realise that children are not passive recipients of knowledge and language but are partners with adults in the co-construction of their realities. Through their interaction with children, adults (and older children) mediate the construction of meaning by helping to create with children the interpersonal conditions within which learning can occur (Cummins, 1994). As has been written elsewhere: "In order for the child to learn, staff must be able to enter the culture of the child, therefore it is important that they see themselves as learners too" (Siraj-Blatchford 1994).

Adults working with young children have the responsibility:

- to create environments in which children feel they can trust and rely on the adults in their lives. "Developing a sense of trust and knowledge that the world is a safe place is central to healthy development in the early years'" (Erikson 1950)
- to foster a sense of belonging in children. This encourages them to explore, experiment and experience their own autonomy
- to enable children to develop a sense of empowerment, which will help them to believe in themselves as competent and capable learners
- to actively promote the diversity of the society we live in. Young children are in the process of learning about who they are as individuals and as members of a broader society
- to actively maintain and develop the home languages of the children. Young bilingual and multilingual children have the right to know that they can continue to use language that encapsulates the important people in their lives, their family, their aspirations, and the knowledge they bring with them to the new environment
- to support parents, value the contribution they make and strive to develop partnerships in the care and education of their children.

Real life voices

Children who are learning English as an additional language discover very quickly that the language they use is not acceptable and that they cannot use it to communicate in the way they have in the first part of their lives, therefore it is important to acknowledge the value of nonverbal communication. Children who are monolingual or come from the mainstream group in the community can be cruel to other children or sometimes over protect them. Early years educators must recognise their responsibility to assist all children to value the use of languages other than English. This includes helping all parents to understand and value multilingualism. Additionally, there is a need for more commitment by governments, both at the local and central level to develop policies and provide adequate resources. It has often been the case that some interpreting systems and structures to assist staff working with minority ethnic children are inadequate and are often too slow to respond to the immediate needs of services and families.

Children learn through feeling good about themselves and if they are anxious they can not learn. Early years practitioners should foster an environment to develop independence and know where resources are available to help children. Often, the ability to respond and understand children who cannot speak English is very poor and many early years educators are not trained adequately, this has a negative impact on children's cognitive development. Practitioners can evaluate practice closely with colleagues through shared observations of individual children and formulate our own strategies (Clarke and Siraj-Blatchford, 1994).

Ideas, themes and questions
In identifying children's powers and adults' responsibilities for living and learning, the following themes must be identified and addressed:
1. Partnerships with parents
2. Valuing diversity for all children
3. Developing policy
4. Responsibilities for educators - including bilingual educators
5. Supporting the self esteem and emotional needs of minority

ethnic children and parents.

Positive partnerships with parents can be achieved when we, as early childhood educators, develop strategies for sharing mutual respect, willingness to negotiate and honesty. Educators must take responsibility for building confidence and getting to know parents as people with a background and views which affect their everyday actions.

There are a number of reasons why it is important to involve parents in the daily life of an early years setting. Each child is an individual and their their language and culture shape their development. Parents can provide valuable information and insights into their children, so that regular discussions with parents can assist staff to become better informed about the child's needs.   In this way a unique curriculum can be developed for each child. Parents have a contribution to make in the planning of the curriculum working towards common goals for their children. This collaboration can result in a more holistic approach. Partnerships build on the contributions that parents can make in the school and other early years settings. The way we respond to parents deserves the same attention and effort as work with children.

It is imperative that we provide an environment that is welcoming, happy, safe and secure and that reflects the community it serves. The environment should be free from ridicule and negative messages which are damaging to any individual regardless of their race, religion, language or culture.

There are a number of ways that educators can work towards positive partnerships with parents:
- provision of multicultural and multilingual material for parents

- training for staff in language awareness
- access to resources which assist staff to learn some words and phrases of other languages
- display of visual images (such as posters and pictures) which depict the diversity of the community
- use of materials which reflect positive images and avoid negative stereotypes
- establishment of parent/ staff working groups.

Parent/staff working groups can provide opportunities for parents to be involved in coffee mornings and discussion groups, cooking sessions, storytelling, group work, outings, fund raising/ideas, sharing musical experiences, celebrating festivals together. When parents participate in the programme/curriculum they can teach staff, carers and educators to be more aware of cultures and languages.

Diversity and multilingualism
Diversity of society should be reflected in all services for young children and needs to be examined in its widest forms, including language, needs, religion, family values, ability, culture, gender, lifestyle, social/economic, human rights.   There are positive benefits for children and families if staff support the diversity of the home languages. All children need to know that their language and culture are accepted and they need to develop a sense of trust and belonging. Staff must assist children to develop positive feelings about themselves and others.

If young children have opportunities to continue the learning of their home language/s in early years settings, the knowledge and experience that these children bring to the centre will be the starting point for their learning in the new environment (Clarke 1992).   This provides the basis for future learning and later achievements.   Additionally, research suggests that bringing children up bilingually can contribute to their cognitive flexibility (Milne and Clarke 1993).

Children need to build on their prior knowledge and experience of the world. This experience and knowledge has been acquired prior to starting in a new environment. All early years experiences for young children should be based on their individual needs and interests. If staff value the diversity of culture, race, and language, their programmes will build on and extend the children's knowledge and experiences. Young bilingual and multilingual children expect that their language and culture will be respected and supported in the centre. All staff in early childhood settings need to have knowledge of the diversity of groups within society.

Equal status of language speakers is an important aspect of all early childhood programmes. Staff members should be seen by children to show respect and to value the diversity of languages in the community. Many languages have dialectic variations. These should be recognised as legitimate ways of speaking. All children must have opportunities to continue their cognitive development, assisted by language. If English is the only language used, then children with language backgrounds other than English are denied access to continued learning until their second language is well established. Young children start in early childhood settings with the basis of their language developed. If these children do not speak English they are not language delayed nor do they have a language disability and English as a second language programmes are different from programmes for language delayed children or children with a language disability (Clarke, 1992)

Equality policies
All early years services should have a written policy which recognises diversity in the community. Policy should include

provision for planning, resources, staffing and training, taking into account social justice practices and employment issues.

It is recognised that we live in a multicultural society. However, this is not necessarily acknowledged by all areas of the community. Not all early years training institutions adequately prepare staff to meet the needs of children and families from diverse backgrounds. All staff need to be adequately trained to cope with the difficult situations that may arise because the values of parents, from different cultural, racial and linguistic backgrounds, sometimes conflict with the values of the mainstream or from the values held by early years staff. In areas of conflict over culture, it is important to remember that human rights take precedent over cultural rights. However, where there is conflict there is always the opportunity for negotiation. For instance, minority ethnic parents may expect their children to learn to read as soon as they go to school. However, many of the children need time to develop English language skills and early years educators need to understand the value of the first language to support the children's development. The awareness of adults in the setting needs to be continually raised.

By valuing all languages we are validating the languages spoken by the community. This gives power back to the language user. There are more people in the world who are bilingual than monolingual. "However, in the British education and care systems being bilingual is still too often perceived as something the children should grow out of" (Siraj-Blatchford 1994).

Responsibilities of adults
The following areas have been identified as important for all early years educators :
1. Individual awareness of the needs, backgrounds and

interests of each child. Educators also need to heighten others' awareness of the needs of minority ethnic children.

2. All educators should be responsible, as individuals and as a group, for keeping issues of race, language, culture and religion alive in the workplace. Items should be included on the agenda of staff meetings and meetings of parents. Attention should also be given to the sharing of the celebration of appropriate festivals.

3. Policies that promote equality should be developed and reviewed regularly. All staff should be committed to implementing these policies and maintaining awareness of the needs of minority ethnic groups in the immediate community, amongst their professional colleagues and with those responsible for funding and delivering services.

4. Parents should be actively involved in the programme, as they are a valuable resource. There are also other local resource agencies in the community, who should be used (such as parent education, health visitors and home/school liaison educators) .

5. Strong networks in local areas can provide early years educators with mutual support. Staff should attend meetings with other providers across a range of sectors; voluntary, private and state, to forge strong links.

6. All educators should recognise that we live in a multicultural society and that fostering bilingualism and multilingualism is important for everyone. If we develop respect for this diversity it will broaden our horizons, encourage the positive aspects of similarities and differences, increase tolerance and understanding and provide opportunities to learn from others. These attitudes need to be communicated to parents.

7. All early years staff need opportunities to attend regular training sessions and programmes. These must focus on issues of race, language, culture and religion and their

relationship to the early years curriculum. Keeping up to date with these issues assists the worker to plan and implement appropriate programmes and assess the needs of individual children in their care.

8. Regular reviews are needed of resources provided in the early years setting. Early years educators need to constantly review resources to update, improve and adapt them if necessary.

9. The programme of the centre should reflect the diversity of the community. Positive images of this diversity should be displayed on the walls of the rooms. Books for the children should be bilingual or available in a range of languages, including English. Children should have the opportunity to hear stories, songs and rhymes in a variety of languages. Parents can assist with recording these on tape.

10. Young children from ethnic minority backgrounds may need longer to settle into the early years curriculum/programme than English speaking children. Educators need to be flexible to respond to each child's individual needs.

11. Early years educators need to make sure that each child's identity is respected. Some practical ways include: spelling and pronouncing the names of the children correctly; always asking permission before using photographs.

Self esteem and emotional needs

A positive self concept is necessary for healthy development and learning and includes feelings about gender, race, ability, culture and language. Positive self-esteem depends on whether children feel that others accept them and see them as competent and worthwhile.   Young children develop attitudes about themselves and others from a very early age and need to be exposed to positive images of diversity in the early years setting. Children need to feel secure and learn to trust the staff that care for them in order to learn effectively.

The following ideas have been suggested as important features of early years programmes:

Home visits
Home visits provide opportunities to make strong links between early years settings and the home. Wherever possible an interpreter should accompany the member of staff to assist with communication. Home visits enable staff to find out more about the children in their care and to observe the dynamics of the family in the cultural environment of the home. This bridge between home and the centre helps staff to learn more about the children in their care. This knowledge enables staff to be sensitive to the children and assists with the settling in time.

Settling in period
The children's settlement into the new environment is more positive when staff are familiar with the environment that the child has come from. If staff have communicated with the new families they are more familiar with the religious and cultural demands upon families and can accommodate them into the programme. Sometimes the children have special dietary needs that need to be respected. If a sense of trust is built up with families this is passed on to the children and helps them become acclimatised to their new environment. There are many different ways of helping families to feel welcomed and secure:
Training and resourcing of staff
- providing opportunities for staff to learn key words in different languages
- building networks to share knowledge and resources with others
- keeping up to date with current issues and knowledge.

Establishing a positive environment
- providing appropriate food in the curriculum based on

cultural and religious needs
- developing positive relationships with children which demonstrate respect, love, security and trust
- establishing a multicultural environment
- selection of staff, board members and governors to represent the diversity in the community

Establish positive links with parents
- developing positive relationships with parents and other family members responsible for the care of children
- sharing in the celebration of appropriate festivals

Establish links with ethnic minority communities
- building links with minority ethnic community leaders
- visiting religious centres

Citizenship
Concepts of citizenship are concerned with attitudes of responsibility both to self and to others. As young children learn about themselves and others within the nursery and in the wider community, the can learn empathy with others. Children can also be encouraged to participate and interact with their environment in an active way. The beginnings of this will be grounded in children being encouraged to participate constructively in activities and experiences within the nursery. Young children can also be involved in making decisions as a group about their environment and participate in democratic processes.   Ideas of democracy have been articulated by, amongst others, Stuart Ranson (1994). Notions of democracy are here linked to the concept of a "learning society in which all are empowered to develop and contribute their capacities" (Ranson, 1993, p.340).   To achieve this vision of society, Ranson argues, it is necessary for people to act as citizens within society, where these citizens are actively involved in making decisions for themselves as individuals and as part of a

wider social structure.   For carers and educators of young children these may seem lofty ideals.   Indeed, as Siraj-Blatchford has expressed it, democracy is an ideal to be worked towards (Siraj-Blatchford, J and I, 1995).

A setting can, however, encourage children to express their views and some discussions about the environment can be held with children. In these pursuits, ideas of active citizenship and democracy are being exercised. It will also be necessary for children to learn that they must act in keeping with group decisions once they have been made and that there may be a tension or conflict between the individuality of each child and the context of the entire nursery. An activity such as collecting waste paper or recyclable material will give children experience of civic participation. It is important that young children within the nursery environment are made to feel part of the wider community, and that, conversely, the wider community is aware of the nursery and the activities of staff and children. Services performed within the community can form part of the learning programme, with local health care educators visiting the nursery to speak to the children.   A topic on health can include discussions on the need for various services and children can go on outings to various places to experience these services first hand.

Important concepts also linked to citizenship are ideas of justice. Children often have a well developed sense of fairness and nursery rules can be explained to young children in terms of notions of justice and fairness of everyone within the setting. It may be possible for some rules to be discussed and negotiated with the children, especially those that directly concern them, such as how many children should be allowed to play in the role play area at any one time, or how time can be allocated on the popular pieces of equipment, such as the bicycles in the outside play area. Solutions to problems and conflicts, which may arise within the nursery, can be analysed and discussed with the children.

Independent learning

Attitudes of self-reliance and self-confidence will be necessary to foster in children. Another important aspect is the notion of children developing as autonomous learners. To achieve this, young children will need to be guided towards the appropriate dispositions for valuing learning and acting independently as learners. It will also be necessary to allow children to experience collaborative learning as part of this process. Creating an environment where children can develop autonomy as learners will involve the adults in the setting responding sensitively to the needs of the children both as individuals and as a cohesive group. Structured programmes are required, but which also allow for flexibility in their implementation. Adults involved with the children will need to be reflective of their own practice and be able to make accurate evaluations about the children and their learning. Assessments of children need to be co-operative ventures, with all members of staff involved in helping to make appropriate meanings from their informal observations and more formal appraisals.

Independent learning is fostered by creating opportunities and experiences which encourage children to use their curiosity and which motivate them. Attitudes of self-reliance and self-confidence are also associated with becoming an independent learner and this is part of an ongoing process of education that stimulates reflection and the development of capabilities and interests. Understandings at this level need to be about encouraging children to make meanings for themselves based on a realisation of how new knowledge may be related to experiences and knowledge they have already gained. Independent learning takes place within an environment that is flexible and responsive to the children. What needs to be understood is that learning is an interactive process among children and between nursery staff and children.

It is important that children are encouraged to take part in making decisions. In this process, staff must give guidance in a meaningful and sensitive way. It will also be important for staff to model the decision making process for children, by thinking aloud when they are themselves seeking solutions to problems. Gradually, children will be able to go through this process themselves and some of the decision making process can be transferred to the children as their skills increase. This transferring of some control is important for children to discover how their efforts can affect their learning. As children develop this understanding, they will acquire greater motivation to continue with their learning. The High/Scope pre-school programme allows children to make decisions about the activities they will engage in and, most importantly, to engage in articulating their decisions and then reviewing them at the end of the session. The latest research concerning adults who followed this programme as children, has shown a greater proportion continuing their education beyond the compulsory number of years than those of their peers who were involved in more formal and didactic early years programmes (Barnett, 1996). This seems to indicate that young children who are exposed to decision-making scenarios early on, continue to be motivated to engage in their own learning.

Independent learning is not carried out in isolation, but will include co-operative small group and large group learning. Independent learners will need to select from a variety of settings, resources and styles to meet their needs and interests. The nursery staff will need to facilitate these different arrangements for learning and actively support them.

Additionally, there needs to be an understanding that to be an effective learner, one will need to take responsibility for one's own learning and that when obstacles are met, perseverance will overcome them. A supportive environment will encourage children to become confident and motivated to learn and they will progress towards greater responsibility for their own learning.

Staff in the nursery setting will be guides, role models and teachers to help the children discover meaning in the activities and experiences that they encounter. Staff will also need to make assessments of children's progress and reflect upon their learning processes. This role is also proactive, as it will allow staff to anticipate difficulties and offer support to children at crucial times.

Staff will also need to enable children to develop thinking skills to aid their learning. These skills can be characterised as a hierarchy of competencies, although children do not learn or progress in hierarchical ways. At the most basic level, children will demonstrate their knowledge and understanding by describing, either verbally or in other ways. At the next level, children apply what they have learned in another place or situation. The next stage is for children to engage in some sort of analysis of the knowledge they have gained and be able to find relationships and categories in which to put information. The fourth level is the ability to make an evaluation by stating an opinion, choice or recommendation. The highest level is being able to synthesise the information and knowledge and hypothesise a scenario or create, compose, design or invent something new.

For example, a child is able to say that the two dimensional shape being shown to her is a square (describing). This same child then notices that the window of the library is square shaped (applying knowledge in another place) and that some other windows are not square because they do not have four sides of equal length and contain four right angles (analysing relationships). Through experiencing squares and other shapes, the child can then make an informed choice of shape to use to make tessellating patterns (evaluating). At the highest level, the child may design a tessellating pattern for wallpaper in the home corner of the nursery (synthesising and creating).

Encouraging and facilitating these thinking skills will give children the tools to be effective learners and problem-solvers, and give them appropriate foundations on which to build their later learning. Together with active social justice practice, notions of democracy, knowledge and understanding for independent learning should be part of a cross-curricular approach to the planning of a nursery programme based on the *Desirable Outcomes.*

Chapter 6

Parent involvement and children's learning

"Not only may the experience at home provide something not readily available in school but also it seems that the skills involved apply as much to the process of attention, perseverance, task performance and work organisation as to particular areas of knowledge. Learning how to learn may be as important as the specifics of what is learned." (Rutter, 1985)

The 1960s and 1970s paved the way for greater parental involvement (Plowden Report, DES, 1967; Taylor Report, DES 1977) in the education of their children, through the assumption that if parents are involved with their child's school then educational progress will be optimised. The term 'partnership' between home and school emerged and since the 1960s parents have been encouraged to participate in many and varied home-school initiatives. In 1985 the DES white paper *Better Schools* restated that parents and schools should become partners in a shared purpose for the benefit of the child, the 1986 Education Act increased parent representation on governing school bodies. The Education Reform Act (DES, 1988) identifies the role of parents as vital to the reform of schools and to the process of raising educational standards through their greater involvement in decision making and the governance of schools.

Home-school initiatives in the last two decades have been many and varied and have changed from being largely compensatory in nature to participatory and inclusive of parents, schools and children (Bastiani, 1988). Parent involvement has been interpreted in a number of ways as: parents in school, as teachers at home, the promotion of home-school links, community education, parents as governors, parents and special educational needs, local and national representation of parents (Wolfendale, 1992; Siraj-Blatchford, 1994; 1995). Wolfendale (1983) claims that parents are their child's prime educators and that they provide:

- the 'primary' (survival) needs
- emotional support and endorsement (secondary) needs
- a setting for personal growth
- the environment for exploration and hypothesis testing
- a frame of reference for exploration outside the home
- a protective environment
- opportunities for independent functioning
- models for language, behaviour etc.
- the transmission of knowledge and information about the world
- arbitration of decisions and decision-makers in the short and long term

Clearly then parents are very important. Some research on parent involvement, for instance many studies in reading and literacy development (Hewison, 1988; Hannon & James, 1990), suggest that children's educational development can be enhanced with long term positive effects. However, other researchers suggest that some forms and patterns of parental involvement can constrain and even contribute towards the reproduction of social inequalities (Mertens & Vass, 1990, Brown, 1994). In working with parents then, this suggests that careful preparation and planning are required.

As has been specified above there have been a number of studies on parent involvement in children's reading progress. Researchers have sought to investigate the reasons for poor reading scores among working class and some minority ethnic groups with a view to improve reading scores and find the strategies which are the most effective. Studies prior to the 1980s suggested that home background did relate to a child's achievement in reading scores based on factors such as socio-economic advantage, parent attitudes and family size. Hewison and Tizard (1980) studied a cohort of working class children to find out which factors made the greatest difference in determining whether a child would learn to read. Whether the mother heard the child read regularly seemed to be much more important than the mother's competence in language or the child's I.Q. A number of studies followed to check this finding.

Hewison (1988) confirmed these findings using an intervention study in a multi-racial inner-city area of London; the gains children made in reading remained three years after the intervention. Other schemes and projects have since proliferated with largely positive outcomes, for instance, the Hackney PACT scheme and paired reading, (Topping and Wolfendale, 1985; Topping, 1992) but it was hard to determine in the latter studies the precise cause of the improvement. Other studies were less successful; for instance, Hannon (1987) conducted a study in Sheffield investigating white working class children's reading achievement when parents and children were encouraged to read books together at home. Little improvement was recorded and Hannon suggests a number of reasons as to why his study was less successful than the Hewison and Tizard study. The two most interesting reasons were the different populations under study. The London children were from multi-ethnic backgrounds and there was less professional involvement in the homes of the Sheffield children. Other studies have shown that teachers' involvement in the home makes a positive impact on reading (Hannon and Jackson, 1987).

Research on school improvement and effectiveness suggests that where staff had been involved in the development of guidelines for their school, there was likely to be school-wide consistency in guideline usage. Where staff had not been involved, however, there was likely to be variation, with teachers tending to adopt individual approaches to the use of guidelines for different curriculum areas. It appears, therefore, that staff involvement was related to a more consistent school-based approach to curriculum. (Mortimore et al, 1988, p233). If we accept that parents are their children's first teachers then it is likely to follow that where there is some consensus and consistency in the home and school's approach to children's learning and the curriculum then more effective learning outcomes can be achieved (Jowett et al., 1991; Long, 1991; Epstein, 1988; 1991; Schaeffer, 1992).

Almost all school improvement and effectiveness studies corroborate that parental involvement is one factor (among several other factors) that improves schools. Rutter et al (1979) argue that school processes are very important to outcomes, and that schools need to consider their ethos as a useful concept in understanding the characteristics of their school as social organisations. Although Rutter et al do not consider the role of parents or parental involvement in any depth it is clearly an area which demands further investigation in its contribution toward creating an ethos that links home and school for the child in a positive way. Rutter et al argue that group influences are powerful and create the norms we begin to take for granted. The combined measure of overall school ethos and process articulated with family processes could provide a stronger cumulative effect on children.

Unlike the United States, where there is a vast literature on school effectiveness, it is only in the last two decades that we have made significant strides in the UK in developing a literature on school improvement and school effectiveness (Reynolds & Cuttance, 1992; Mortimore et al., 1988; Smith &

Tomlinson, 1989; MacBeath, 1994). It is even more recent that any attention has been paid to the effects on schools of educational reform since the introduction of the National Curriculum (Bowe et al., 1992; MacBeath, 1994; Siraj-Blatchford, 1994; Hughes, 1994; Barber, 1995). However, there is a substantive gap in British literature on studies of school improvement through parental involvement. In the United States the large-scale and longitudinal studies conducted by Joyce Epstein (Brandt, 1989; Epstein, 1987; 1988; Epstein & Dauber, 1991) offer a useful model (below) upon which investigations of school and nursery improvement (particularly those aimed at raising the academic achievement of pupils) and parental involvement can be explored.

Five Types of Parent Involvement is seen as important:
1. Parenting skills, child development, and home environment for learning.
2. Communications from school to home.
3. Parents as volunteers in school.
4. Involvement in learning activities at home.
5. Decision making, leadership, and governance.

(Epstein, 1988)

Recent governments have been increasingly concerned to foster parental choice and participation in the process of their children's education. This concern has largely been manifested through the Education Reform Act (1988) which applies to the statutory school sector. Parents have, in line with market philosophy, more `choice' in selecting the school that their child attends and a right to regular reports on academic achievement. In response to a perceived failure of schools to inform and involve parents, the previous government issued a parent's charter outlining the rights that parents have been given. Parents are seen as the prime clients of the education service and therefore schools are accountable to them. However, a partnership aimed at developing a complementary role in educating the child is less obvious.

Julia Gilkes (1989), in her book *Developing Nursery Education,* describes how one nursery school worked towards gaining the trust of families in the white, working-class community in Kirkby. Gilkes explains how parents were encouraged to be involved in the school. In some cases this meant teachers first supporting the parents and their children in many ways and for several years before the parents felt ready to come forward. Parents had first to feel supported, helped and valued before they could reciprocate by participating in a partnership sense. This principle probably applies to most early years settings: parents first and foremost need to feel that the setting offers them something, such as friendship, advice, regular reports on their child's progress, support or even just a chance to have coffee and meet other parents and carers. What Gilkes (1989) is really saying is that schools and nurseries have to get their ethos right. A supportive, even therapeutic, setting is one that creates confidence in those who has a stake in it.

An atmosphere or ethos that encourages a sense of belonging should aim to:
- make everyone feel that they are wanted and that they have a positive role to play in the early years setting;
- show parents that they can always make their feelings, views and opinions known to the staff, and that these will be dealt with respectfully and seriously;
- demonstrate that the parents' linguistic, cultural and religious backgrounds are valued and seen as positive assets to the setting, and
- show that the setting is an organic part of the community it serves and so understands the concerns, aspirations and difficulties the members of that community might face.

The Children Act (Volume 2, 1989), states that parents of young children have certain parental rights, which allow them to influence the quality of education and care their child receives. They should be able to acquire information about the early years setting, choose between settings, and modify, express views about and contribute to their child's learning. This has serious implications for parents who are not confident about using English. Early years educators need to ensure that they offer the whole community an equal chance to understand and use their service. If this means translating notices about the setting and putting them in areas where minority ethnic families will see them, for example doctors' surgeries, then this should be taken as a first step to ensure initial interest.

Parents are not a homogeneous group and therefore can hold different culturally conceived ideas about the role of education and the teacher. In some cultures the role of the teacher is seen as distinct and separate to the role of parenting, and early years practitioners need to take some time explaining and illustrating how the child can benefit from partnership and continuity of educational experiences across school and home. It is important for staff not to make assumptions about parents' knowledge, beliefs or experiences, but to create a friendly atmosphere where parents can talk openly about their experiences and feelings. Additionally, sufficient interest should be taken in each parent as an individual and their views and feelings should be sought on general matters pertaining to the setting and particularly to their child. This sort of interest and care fosters trust and an open and secure ambience.

In the process of providing information and establishing a partnership it is staff who must take the lead responsibility as they are the ones with the power. It may not feel that way to individual staff, particularly those who have less paper qualifications or are on part-time contracts, but to the parents they represent the 'establishment', with the `voice' that counts. All staff can work towards partnership by creating an ethos of belonging to the setting. This ethos can be characterised by:

- regular and effective communication;
- willingness to share information with parents about their child and the nursery;
- willingness to ask parents for advice about their child and to seek their views on key issues such as curriculum, child rearing and assessment;
- working towards common goals, taking time to explain and listen carefully;
- visibly displaying a liking for parents and respect for their feelings;
- being approachable and open to negotiation;
- sharing responsibility and a willingness to work together, and
- illustrating that the child is at the heart of the education provided and therefore that the care/family unit is all-important.

A booklet or parent guide (if required, in the appropriate community languages) can make these points clearly and succinctly. But there is no substitute for a warm and caring reception from staff at the early years setting. For parents who are very busy, and particularly black and minority ethnic parents some of whom may be illiterate in English and in their own language, the only medium for understanding the school may be through personal contact. This certainly applies to only a minority, and not most parents, but these are the parents that staff should particularly be communicating with.

In summary home links or parent involvement is a component of effective early years settings that merits special consideration. When it is well planned it can promote higher success in pupils and lead to more successful family environments. Many studies have shown that when parents, teachers and children collaborate towards the same goals it leads to improved academic performance of pupils. Schools also report that children show a more positive attitude towards learning and are better behaved (Tizard et al, 1982; Hannon, 1990; Hewison, 1988). Research also suggests that home-school communication leads to better understanding and more positive attitudes by teachers and parents about each other's roles.

When combined with a quality curriculum, parent involvement has been shown to be one of the most potent ingredients in producing high quality early years education (see High/Scope evidence in Schweinhart et al 1993) for young children. We hope that this book has triggered deeper interest in both and a validation of the good practice which already exists. We also hope that any part of the book which challenges practitioners will also be met with the same degree of interest.

References

Ahlberg, A. and Ahlberg, J. (1977), *Each Peach Pear Plum*, London: Puffin.

Athey, C. (1990), *Extending Thought in Young Children*, London: Paul Chapman.

The Audit Commission (1996), *Counting to Five: Education of Children Under Five*, London: HMSO.

Ball, S. J. (1990), *Politics and Policy Making in Education*, London: Routledge.

Ball, S. J. (1994), *Education Reform: A Critical and Post-structural Approach*, Milton Keynes: The Open University Press.

Bash, L. and Coulby, D, (eds), (1989), *The Education Reform Act: Competition and Control*, London: Cassell.

Barnett, W. S. (1996), *Lives in the Balance: Age-27 Benefit-Cost Analysis of the High/Scope Perry Pre-school Program (Monographs of the High/Scope Educational Research Foundation, 11)*, Ypsilanti, MI: High/Scope Press.

Blenkin, G.M., Hurst, V.M., Whitehead, M.R., and Yue, N.Y.L. (1995), *Principles into practice: improving the quality of children's early learning: Phase 1 report*, London: Goldsmiths College.

Blenkin, G.M. and Kelly, A.V. (eds) (1996), *Early Childhood Education: A Developmental Curriculum*, London: Chapman.

Bowe, R. and Ball, S. J. (1992) *Reforming Education and Changing Schools*, London: Routledge.

Brown, C. (1993), 'Bridging the gender gap in science and technology: How long will it take?', *International Journal of Technology and Design Education*, Vol 3, No.2, pp.65-73.

Browne, A. (1996), *Developing Language and Literacy 3-8*, London: Paul Chapman.

Buchanan, K. (1995), 'Aims, beliefs, practices and training of early childhood practitioners from three different backgrounds' in *International Journal of Early Childhood*, October 1995, pp.1-9.

Bussis, A., Chittenden, E. A., Amarel, M. (1976), *Beyond Surface Curriculum*, Colarado: Westview Press

Calgren, I., Handal, G. and Vaage, J. (eds) (1994), *Teachers' Minds and Actions: Research on Teachers' Thinking and Practice*, London: Falmer Press.

Carr, M. and May, H. (1993), 'Choosing a model. Reflecting on the development and process of Te Whariki: National Early Childhood Curriculum Guidelines in New Zealand' in *International Journal of Early Years Education*, Vol. 1, No. 3, pp. 7-21.

Charlesworth, R., Hart, C.H., Burts, D.C., Hernandez, S. (1991), 'Kindergarten teachers beliefs and practices' in *Early Child Development and Care*, 70, pp.17-35.

Clarke, P.M. (1992), *English as a 2nd Language in early childhood*, Vic: Free Kindergarten Association.

Clarke, P.M. and Siraj-Blatchford, I. (1994), 'Bilingual and Multilingual Children', paper presented at the National Children's Bureau biannual conference in Nottingham.

Clarke, S. (1995), 'Assessing significant achievement in the primary classroom', *British Journal of Curriculum and Assessment*, pp.12-16.

Cummins. J. 'Knowledge, power, and identity in teaching English as second language' in Genesee, F. (1994), *Educating Second Language Children. The whole child, the whole curriculum, the whole community*, Cambridge: Cambridge University Press .

Department for Education (1992), *Choice and Diversity: A New Framework for Schools*, London: HMSO.

Department for Education and Employment (1997), *Early years development partnerships and early years development plans for 1998/1999: draft guidance for consultation*, London: HMSO.

Department for Education and Employment (1997), *Progress with Partnerships*, London: HMSO.

Department of Education and Science (1990), *Starting with Quality*, London: HMSO.

Derman-Sparks, L. (1989), *Anti-Bias Curriculum*, Washington DC: NAEYC

Drummond, M.J. (1993), *Assessing Children's Learning*, London: David Fulton.

Edwards, C., Gandini, L. and Forman, G. (1993), *The Hundred Languages of Children: The Reggio Emilia Approach to Early Childhood Education*, New Jersey: Ablex Publishing Corporation.

Erikson, E.H. (1950), *Childhood and Society*, Norton.

Fitz, J., Halpin, D., Power, S. (1994), 'Implementation research and education policy: practice and prospects' in *British Journal of Educational Studies* XXXXII:1, pp.53-69.

Gammage, P. and Meighan, J. (eds) (1995), *Early Childhood Education: The Way Forward*, Derby: Education Now.

Gipps, C. and Stobart, G. (1993), *Assessment: A Teachers Guide to the Issues*, London: Hodder and Stoughton.

Goldschmeid, E. and Jackson, S. (1994), *People Under Three*, London: Routledge.

Goodson, I.F., and Hargreaves, A. (1996), *Teachers' Professional Lives*, London: Falmer Press.

Hatch, J.A. and Freeman, E. B. (1988), 'Kindergarten philosophies and practices: perspectives of teachers, principals and supervisors' in *Early Childhood Research Quarterly*, 3, pp.151-166.

Hohmann, M., Barnet, B. and Weikart, D.P. (1979), *Young Children in Action*, Ypsilanti: High/Scope Press.

Honig, A.S. (1983), 'Sex role socialization in early childhood', *Young Children*, 38(6), pp.57-70.Hurst, V. (1991), 'Examining the emperors new clothes: nursery practitioners and the nursery curriculum in the post-1988 climate' in *Early Years* 15:1, pp.37-41.

Hutchin, V. (1996), *Tracking Significant Achievement in the Early Years*, London: Hodder and Stoughton.

Isenberg, J.P., Renck Jalengo, M. (eds) (1997), *Major Trends and Issues in Early Childhood Education*, New York: Teachers College Press.

Katz, L.G. (1995), *Talks with Teachers of Young Children: A Collection*, New Jersey: Ablex Publishing Corporation.

Katz, L.G. (1982), 'Development of children's racial awareness and intergroup attitudes' *Current topics in early childhood education*, Vol. 4 pp.17-54, Norwood, NJ: Ablex.

Le Grand, J. and Bartlett, R. (1993), *Quasi Markets and Social Policy*, London: MacMillan.

Lally, M, (1991), *The Nursery Teacher in Action*, London: Paul Chapman.

Maccoby, E.E. (ed) (1966), *The Development of Sex Differences*, Stanford, CA: Stanford University Press.

Macleod, F. (ed), (1989), *The High/Scope Project*, Exeter: School of Education.

Makins, V. (1997), *Not Just A Nursery: Multi-agency Early Years Centres in Action*, London: NCB.

Milner, D (1983), *Children and Race: 10 Years On*, Ward Lock Educational

Milne, R. and Clarke, P.(1993), *Bilingual Early Childhood Education in Child Care and Preschool Centres*, Vic: Free Kindergarten Association.

Ministry of Education (1996), *Te Whariki: Early Childhood Curriculum*, Wellington: Learning Media Limited.

Morgan, M. (1988), *Art 4-11:Art in the Early Years of Schooling*, Oxford, Blackwell.

Moriarty, V. (1997), *Responses of Early Years Educators to the Desirable Outcomes for Children's Learning*, unpublished MA dissertation, University of London Institute of Education.

Moriarty, V. (1998) 'Early Childhood Educators' Perceptions of the UK Desirable Outcomes for Children's Learning: A research study on the policy implications' *International Journal of Early Childhood Education*, Vol. 30, No 1 pp. 56-64

Moss, P. and Pence, A. (1994), *Valuing Quality in Early Childhood Services*, London: Paul Chapman.

Moss, P. and Penn, H.(1996), *Transforming Nursery Education*, London: Paul Chapman.

Pascal, C., Betram, T. and Ramsden, F. (1997), 'The Effective Early Learning Research Project: Reflections upon the action during Phase 1', in *Early Years*, 17, 2, pp.40-47.

Penn, H. (1994), 'Comparing concepts of learning in publicly funded day nurseries in Italy, Spain and Britain' in *International Journal of Early Years Education*, 2:3, pp.54-67.

Pound, L. (1989), 'You can always tell a good nursery by its ammunition boxes: intentions underlying practice in nursery schools and classes' in *Early Child Development and Care*, 49, pp.75-90.

Ranson, S. (1993), 'Markets or democracy for education' in British Journal of Educational Studies, Vol XXXXI, No. 4, pp.333-352.

Ranson, S. (1994), *Towards the Learning Society*, London: Cassell.

School Curriculum and Assessment Authority (1996), *Nursery Education Scheme: The Next Steps*, London: HMSO.

School Curriculum and Assessment Authority (1996), *Baseline Assessment: Draft Proposals*, London: HMSO.

Schweinhart, L.J., Barnes, H.V. and Weikart, D.P. (1993), *Significant Benefits: The High/Scope Perry Pre-school Project Through Age 27,* USA: High/Scope Education Research Foundation

Schweinhart, L.J. and Weikart, D.P. (1997), 'The High/Scope Pre-school curriculum comparison study through Age 23, in *Early Childhood Research Quarterly*, 12, pp.117-143).

Scottish Office Education Department (1996), *Using Performance Indicators in Nursery Schools/Class/Pre-Five Unit*, Scottish Education Department.

Siraj-Blatchford, I (1992) 'Why understanding cultural difference is not enough' in Pugh, G. (ed), *Contemporary Issues in the Early Years*, London: Paul Chapman Publishers.

Siraj-Blatchford, I. (1993) `Educational Research and Reform: Some Implications for the Professional Identity of Early Years Teachers'. *British Journal of Educational Studies*, XXX1, 4, 398-408.

Siraj-Blatchford, I. (1994), *The Early Years: Laying the Foundations for Racial Equality*,Stoke-on-Trent: Trentham Books.

Siraj-Blatchford, J. and I. (eds) (1995) *Educating the Whole Child: Cross-curricular Skills, Themes and Dimensions*, Buckingham: Open University Press.

Siraj-Blatchford, I. (1995) 'Expanding Combined Nursery Provision: Bridging the Gap between Care and Education' in Gammage & Meighan (Eds) *Early Childhood Education: The Way Forward.* Nottingham: Education Now Books

Siraj-Blatchford, I. (ed.) (1998) *A Curriculum Development Handbook for Early Childhood Educators.* Stoke-on-Trent: Trentham Books

Spodek, B. (1987), 'Thought processes underlying preschool teachers' classroom decisions' in *Early Child Development and Care*, 29, pp.197-208.

Spodek, B. (1988), 'The implicit theories of early childhood teachers' in *Early Child Development and Care*, 38, pp.13-32.

Spodek, B. and Saracho, O. (eds) (1991), *Issues in Early Childhood Curriculum*, New York: Teachers College Press.

Sylva, K. and Moss, P. (1992), *Learning Before School*, NCE Briefing No. 8, London: National Commission on Education

Sylva, K., Siraj-Blatchford, I., (1995), *Bridging the Gap Between Home and School: Improving Achievement in Primary Schools*, UNESCO.

Sylva, K., Siraj-Blatchford, I., Johnson, S. (1992), 'The impact of the UK National Curriculum on pre-school practice. Some top-down processes at work' in *International Journal of Early Childhood*, 24, pp.41-51.

Tizard, B. and Hughes, M. (1984), *Young Children Learning: Talking and Thinking at Home and at School*, London: Fontana.

Vygotsky, L. (1978), *Mind in Society*, Cambridge: Harvard University Press.

Warnock Committee (1978), *Report of the Committee of Enquiry into Special Educational Needs*, London: HMSO.

Wells, G. (1986), *The Meaning Makers: Children Learning Language and Using Language To Learn,* Portsmouth NH: Heinemann.

Whalley, M. (1994), *Learning to be Strong*, Kent: Hodder and Stoughton.

Whalley, M. (1997), *Working with Parents*, London: Hodder and Stoughton.

Whitehead, M (1990), *Language and Literacy in the Early Years*, London: Paul Chapman.

Wong-Fillmore, L. (1991), 'A question for early childhood programmes. English first or families first?' in *Education Week*, June 1991. pp32.

Wylie, C. (1996), *Five Years Old and Competent*, Wellington, NZ: New Zealand Council for Educational Research.

Woodhead, M. (1996), *In Search of the Rainbow*, Den Haag: Bernard Van Leer Foundation.

United Nations (1959) Declaration of the Rights of the Child.

Index

EDUCATION NOW PUBLICATIONS

Books:

Early Childhood Education: The Way Forward
edited by Philip Gammage and Janet Meighan £9-95
Essential reading for all involved in the education of young children.

Issues in Early Childhood Education
by Philip Gammage and Rosalind Swann £3-95

Learning Technology, Science and Social Justice: an integrated approach for 3-13 year olds by John Siraj-Blatchford £13-95

Can You Teach Creativity? by Anna Craft et.al. £11-95
We need a new approach for fostering creativity and vision

Developing Democratic Education edited by Clive Harber £9-95
Democracy is not genetic - it is learned behaviour, but schools are currently organised on anti-democratic principles.

Beyond Authoritarian School Management by Lynn Davies £9-95
How to move beyond the limitations of authoritarian school management into more effective forms of practice

Learning From Home-based Education ed. Roland Meighan £4-95
...the rich diversity of the home-based phenomenon is demonstrated.

Praxis Makes Perfect: Critical Educational Research for Social Justice by Iram Siraj-Blatchford £6-95

The Further Education Curriculum by Anna Frankel et.al. £9-50
The Modernity of Further Education by Frank Reeves £9-50
Further Education and Economic Regeneration ed Frank Reeves £9-50
Further Education and Democracy by Keith Wymer £9-50

News and Review is the quarterly publication which promotes the vision and ideas of *Education Now* Subscription £20 Per Annum

....

Information Packs available *Home-based Education,* on *Flexi-time Schooling,* and on *The Next Learning System* at £10-00 each

....

Full list from: **Education Now, 113 Arundel Drive, Bramcote Hills, Nottingham NG9 3FQ** Tel/fax 0115 925 7261